Landscapes of the
COSTA
BRAVA
and Barcelona

a countryside guide
Second edition

Michael Lockwood
and
Teresa Farino

Second edition © 2006
Sunflower Books™
PO Box 36160
London SW7 3WS, UK
www.sunflowerbooks.co.uk

Published in the USA by
Hunter Publishing Inc
130 Campus Drive
Edison, NJ 08818
www.hunterpublishing.com

ISBN 1-85691-303-1

The church at Mura (Car tour 1)

Important note to the reader

We have tried to ensure that the descriptions and maps in this book are error-free at press date. The book will be updated, where necessary, whenever future printings permit. It will be very helpful for us to receive your comments (sent in care of the publishers, please) for the updating of future printings.

We also rely on those who use this book — especially walkers — to take along a good supply of common sense when they explore. Conditions can change fairly rapidly on the Costa Brava, and *storm damage or bulldozing may make a route unsafe at any time*. If the route is not as we outline it here, and your way ahead is not secure, return to the point of departure. *Never attempt to complete a tour or walk under hazardous conditions!* Please read carefully the notes on pages 50 to 58, as well as the introductory comments at the beginning of each tour and walk (regarding road conditions, equipment, grade, distances and time, etc). Explore *safely*, while at the same time respecting the beauty of the countryside.

Cover photograph: Madremanya (Car tour 4)
Title page: Escher's blue (Polyommatus escheri)

Photographs: pages 8, 24 (bottom), 38 (right), 40, 44 (top right and bottom), 68, 69, 76 (all), 88 (right-hand column, bottom two), 89, 96 (right), 97 (all), 112, 132: Teresa Farino; page 41: Constantí Stefanescu; all other photographs: Michael Lockwood
Maps: John Underwood
A CIP catalogue record for this book is available from the British Library.
Printed and bound in England: J H Haynes & Co Ltd
10 9 8 7 6 5 4 3 2

❀ Contents

4   Landscapes of the Costa Brava and Barcelona

❃ Preface

It's become something of a cliché that there's much more to Spain — and in the case of this book, Catalonia — than the beaches so relentlessly promoted by the package-holiday travel agencies. Today, people are increasingly aware that somewhere inland there lies a fascinating country just waiting to be explored. And yet this new knowledge is, in many cases, ultimately frustrating, since so little has been published — other than in very general guidebooks — on where to go for a quiet day's walking and wildlifing in and around the major holiday destinations of Barcelona and the Costa Brava.

Strictly speaking, the Costa Brava — literally the 'rugged coast', in reference to the rocky, inhospitable nature of much of the shore — runs from the French border southwards to the town of Blanes, 60km north of Barcelona, also encompassing the bird-rich coastal marshes of the Aiguamolls de l'Empordà. Further south, between Blanes and Barcelona, the flat coastal plain is largely devoted to market gardening and resort-based tourism, while the abruptness of the Garraf Massif (Walk 1), plunging directly into the Mediterranean just south of Barcelona, has largely precluded abusive tourist development (although not large-scale quarrying).

Behind the coast lies a jumble of ill-defined mountain ranges that is really nothing more than a collection of geolo-

Puigsacalm and Puig Corneli rise behind the village of Joanetes (Walks 9, 10)

gically, ecologically and scenically very disparate ridges and peaks that forms a rough chain drifting south from the eastern end of the Pyrenees towards the tail of the Iberian mountains, way down the coast in Tarragona. Known as the Serralada Litoral and Serralada Prelitoral, these ranges include such varied landscapes as the extraordinary conglomerate pinnacles of Montserrat, the dormant volcanoes of the Garrotxa and the subalpine heights of the Montseny. It is this very variety, coupled with its proximity to Barcelona and the coastal towns, that makes the hinterland of the Costa Brava so attractive to walkers.

The Catalans are great recreational walkers and the local tradition of *excursionisme* is as much linked to the variety of scenery on offer as to the political fact of the long years — 1939 to 1975 — of Franco's dictatorship. Firstly, the beckoning peaks, often snow-clad, the thick, verdant forests and the rugged cliffs with their hidden trails — 'monks' paths', as we like to call them — simply *invite* exploration, while secondly, since Franco's regime banned the use of Catalan, the one place people could go to chatter freely in their native tongue was, precisely, the countryside, far from the *Guardia Civil* who could fine people for speaking Catalan rather than Castilian Spanish.

In the 21st century, in times of relative democracy, those of us lucky enough to visit the Catalan countryside will find ourselves immersed in a predominantly rural society in which the *masia* — the isolated but generally self-sufficient farmhouse — still plays a major role. For centuries, the occupants of these architecturally noble buildings had to resort to taking the shortest route on foot (only the rich could afford a horse) whenever it was necessary to visit the neighbours or go to market. Nowadays, most *pagesos* — literally, 'peasants', but in Catalan a respectful term to describe those who live off the land — now have cars and tractors, although for every ostensibly efficient, large 'hi-tec' farm, there are still many small, isolated *masies*, operating at a very low-key, virtually subsistence level. Nevertheless, as you will discover during your walks, the phenomenon of rural-urban drift is prompting the gradual abandonment of the *masies*, such that many of these ancient trails and footpaths are becoming overgrown. Thanks to the efforts of the numerous *clubs d'excursionistes* that exist throughout Catalonia, however, a substantial number are now waymarked with cairns, paint-marks and, increasingly, by accurate signposts. This is not to imply, however, that a virgin, rural hinterland awaits the walker who escapes the confines of beach or city.

The 19th century saw the Catalan bourgeoisie build their country retreats in such attractive localities as El Figaró (Walk 5) while, more recently, *urbanitzacions* (sprawling complexes of detached weekend houses for city folk) have been springing up in the middle of nowhere like so many mushrooms. Add to the equation centuries of deforestation, forest fires, road-building and quarrying, and you will see that, unfortunately, it isn't just a question of stopping the car or getting off the train at random and starting walking; you need guidance to find the best routes.

As far as possible, we have tried to describe here the *best* walks in this part of Catalonia, be they the classic, well-waymarked routes that form part of the repertoire of any self-respecting Catalan walker, or some of our personal favourites way off the beaten track. In the first instance, you will *always* meet other ramblers at weekends on Walks 6 and 7, although possibly not midweek, but by contrast, Walks 5, 8 and 22 will *never* be busy, even on the finest spring Sunday.

Because we are keen naturalists, many of the walks described in this book will draw your attention to the enormous variety of wildlife on offer, and we urge you to carry a pair of binoculars and the appropriate field guides. During the course of your forays into rural Catalonia, we hope you will learn that a three-hour walk can also take six hours, especially in spring, when the limestone hills are teeming with orchids, or in summer, when the flower-rich waysides are alive with nectaring butterflies.

Acknowledgements

The authors would like to thank all those anonymous workers in information centres who patiently answered our in-numerable questions, as well as those who offered suggestions on routes or made the often solitary task of finding the right path so much more enjoyable with their company. In purely alphabetical order those people are as follows: Andrew Alcock, Guillem Alcock, John Coltrane, Sergi Herrando, Elena Rincón, Xavi Rincón, Isabel Roura, Andreu Salvat, Ottobrina Voccoli, Toby Willett and Bob Wills. Above all, however, this book is dedicated to Las Hermanas Orellana and '*la nena*', who ensured that it had a happy ending.

Useful books

Although many general and walking guides exist in Catalan and Spanish, very little has been published in any other language. Overleaf is a list of just some of the more recom-mendable books available in English.

General guides

Brown, J (1994) *Barcelona and Catalunya*. The Rough Guides, London

Departament de Cultura de la Generalitat de Catalunya (1993) *This is Catalonia — A Guide to its Architectural Heritage*. Generalitat de Catalunya

Simonis, D (2001) *Catalunya and the Costa Brava*. Lonely Planet

Williams, R (ed.) (1991) *Insight Guides: Catalonia*. APA Publications (UK) Ltd

Background reading

Hooper, J (1987) *The Spaniards — A Portrait of the New Spain*. Penguin, London. Contains interesting sections on Catalonia.

Hughes, R (1993) *Barcelona*. Vintage, New York. The best history of the city in English.

Lewis, N (1984) *Voices of the Old Sea*. Penguin, London. A fascinating view of the Costa Brava in the 1950s.

Wild peony (Paeonia officinalis)

Field guides in English

Flora

Polunin, O and Smythies, B E (1973) *Flowers of South-west Europe — a field guide*. Oxford University Press. The most complete guide in a single volume.

Grey-Wilson, C and Blamey, M (1979) *Alpine Flowers of Britain and Europe*. Collins, London. Good for walks above 1000m.

Blamey, M and Grey-Wilson, C (1993) *Mediterranean Wild Flowers*. HarperCollins, London. This includes almost all the plants found on the lower walks.

Birds

Mullarney, K, Svensson, L, Zetterström, D and Grant, P J (1999) *Collins Bird Guide*. HarperCollins, London. The best of its ilk — indispensable!

Butterflies

Tolman, T and Lewington, R (1997) *Butterflies of Britain and Europe*. HarperCollins, London. Excellent drawings, slightly scanty text.

Chinery, M (1998) *A Photographic Guide to the Butterflies of Britain and Europe*. HarperCollins, London. The best photo-guide by a long way, with a more complete text than the previous book.

Other groups

Macdonald, D and Barrett, P (1993) *Collins Field Guide to the Mammals of Britain and Europe*. HarperCollins, London

Arnold, E N and Burton, J A (1999) *A Field Guide to the Reptiles and Amphibians of Britain and Europe*. HarperCollins, London

Chinery, M (1993) *Insects of Britain and Western Europe*. HarperCollins, London

d'Aguilar, J, Dommanget, J-L and Préchac, R (1986) *A Field Guide to the Dragonflies of Britain, Europe and North Africa*. Collins, London

Farino, T and Lockwood, M (2003) *Travellers' Nature Guide: Spain*. Oxford University Press. Contains detailed information about the natural history of the places mentioned in this book.

Nearby 'Landscapes' from Sunflower

Jenner, P and Smith, C (4th edition, 2005) *Landscapes of the Pyrenees*

Underwood, J and P (2nd edition, 2004) *Landscapes of Western Provence and Languedoc-Roussillon*

Getting about

Catalonia is blessed with a fairly extensive public transport system, and many of the walks in this book can be reached using buses and trains.

Catalonia has *two* **rail** networks: the Spanish state system **RENFE** (www.renfe.es) and the narrow-gauge **Ferrocarrils de la Generalitat** (**FGC**; www.fgc.net). All the RENFE trains serving Walks 1 and 5 and connecting with the bus for Walk 4 pass through Barcelona and stop at the **Estació de Sants** (the central station); for Walk 1 trains also stop at the **Passeig de Gràcia** station, while for Walks 4 and 5, trains also stop at the **Plaça de Catalunya** station. RENFE trains heading northeast towards Girona, Figueres and the Costa Brava depart from the Estació de Sants then pass through the Passeig de Gràcia. The FGC network also has more than one station in Barcelona: Walk 2 is served by trains heading towards Terrassa or Sabadell from a station in **Plaça Catalunya**, whereas Walk 3 is reached from a station in the **Plaça d'Espanya**, from which trains depart towards Manresa (line R5) to connect with the cable car up to Montserrat.

Bus companies are legion, serving most towns and large villages, although in more remote rural areas many only provide a weekday service for school children and/or a once-a-week service for shoppers heading to the local market. These are thus of little use to walkers as they head towards the nearest large town in the morning and return to the hills in the afternoon.

Three major companies serve most of the area covered by this book: **Sagalès** ((93 2312756; www.sagales.com), covering Barcelona and its hinterland; **Sarfa** ((902 302025; www.sarfa.com), serving the area between Figueres, Girona and the Costa Brava; and **Teisa** ((93 2153566; www.teisa-bus.com/web/llistah.htm), operating in La Garrotxa. Timetables should be available in the tourist information offices of the major towns: in **Barcelona** this is located at Palau Robert 107, Passeig de Gràcia; in **Girona** at Rambla de la Llibertat 1, and in **Figueres** in the Plaça del Sol.

The timetables printed on the back of the touring map cover most of the public transport options used in this book (the remainder are described in individual walks), but obviously are subject to change. Rail timetables are apt to be altered in May, to adjust to summer demand, and then again in September. **Important**: *do* check bus/train times before embarking on any walks, and *always* put out your hand to stop a bus, even if you are standing at a recognised bus stop.

Taxis are available even in quite small towns and should have an established fare for a standard route from one town to another. Prices are reasonable, and taxis are a good option for Walks 9 and 10 (taxi from Olot) and Walks 18 and 19 (taxi from Roses or Castelló d'Empúries); for Walk 20, a taxi is almost indispensable. Be sure to check fares *before* you commit yourself; a small tip is usually considered appropriate.

When all's said and done, however, a **car** is undoubtedly the most convenient option, both for exploring some of the more remote valleys in this part of Catalonia and for accessing some of the walks; private transport is *essential* for Walks 7, 21, 22 and 23. Car hire is available at both Barcelona and Girona airports, in larger towns such as Figueres and in the busier coastal resorts. Roads have improved beyond all recognition during the past decade, but be prepared for traffic jams on Friday afternoons/evenings, Saturday mornings and on the eve of public holidays on major roads leading out of Barcelona, and then again on Sunday evenings or after a holiday heading back into the city. The main roads around the Costa Brava, for example Roses to Figueres or Palafrugell to Girona, can also be very busy at peak periods.

View over Sant Pere de Rodes towards Port de la Selva from near the Castell de Sant Salvador de Verdera (Short walk 16 for motorists; Car tour 6)

● Short walks and picnic suggestions

Travelling through rural Catalonia, the opportunities for short walks and picnics are almost limitless, given the abundance of stunning viewpoints and shady springs. In the car tours we have highlighted 18 *essentially short, easy walks for motorists* — ideal opportunitites for you to stretch your legs en route to a particularly scenic spot for a picnic, or to investigate the wildlife of rural Catalonia without having to undertake a full walk. Look for the 🚗 symbol on the fold-out touring map, followed by the appropriate number.

The maximum length of these short walks is just 6km/3.7mi, but many are much shorter, and climbing has been kept to a minimum. No individual maps are provided for these short routes, but several of them coincide with parts of the main walks (if so, a page reference is given for the appropriate map). Most of these routes are linear, so you can shorten the walk even further by turning back at any point. *Appropriate equipment* for all these walks is the same: stout shoes, sunhat, cardigan, raingear, picnic and water. Don't forget to read the country code overleaf before you start.

For reasons of space, we have been able to mention only a few of our favourite roadside picnic spots at the start of the car tours (marked with a *P* in the touring notes and on the touring map). Other possibilities are highlighted in the short walks for motorists, and good picnic spots are also mentioned towards the start of most of the main walks.

Catalan cuisine ranges from seafood, fish, salads and rice dishes near the coast to a carbohydrate-rich diet dominated by pulse stews and local meats in more montane inland areas. Nevertheless, some believe that the real star of Catalan cuisine is the ubiquitous *pa amb tomàquet* (bread with tomato) — which is nothing more than fleshy, mature tomatoes rubbed into bread, the whole drizzled with olive oil and sprinkled with salt — a meal in itself, especially if it is accompanied by some cheese or cold meat. A variant on the theme involves toasting the bread first, then rubbing it with a clove of raw garlic before adding the other ingredients.

Most villages have a bakery (opening hours vary), where you can purchase either a *barra* (a French-style loaf) or *pa de*

11

pagès (a large round loaf which the baker will slice up for you). Local markets (market days are detailed in the car tours) and most supermarkets stock a bewildering array of local cheeses (the goats'-milk ones are especially good) and *embotit*, the latter term encompassing all manner of cold pork sausages, some of the more commonplace of which are *xoriço, saltxitxó, llonganissa, bull, botifarra negra* and *botifarra blanca*. Good fresh fruit is readily available; look out for loquats in May, a myriad varieties of succulent peaches in July, and fresh figs and custard apples in late summer.

Countryside code

The experienced walker is accustomed to following a 'country code' when walking, but the casual visitor may not have the necessary knowledge to avoid causing damage to property or livestock, and may even endanger his or her own life.

- **AVOID TAKING RISKS**: This is the most important point of all. Do *not* attempt walks beyond your ability and do not wander off the route described in this book if there is any sign of mist or if it is late in the day.
- **Do not walk alone**, and always tell a responsible person where you are going and at what time you plan to return.
- **Only light fires** at picnic areas equipped with fireplaces or barbecue facilities. Forest fires are a constant threat in lowland Catalonia in summer, and the making of fires outside the specified areas is prohibited from March to October. Cigarette ends must be disposed of with care; motorists can be fined for throwing them out of the car window,
- **Respect all animals**. Stock-rearing is a way of life in rural Catalonia, and farmers will respect you if you respect their animals. The livestock you meet on your walks is not necessarily tame. By making loud noises or trying to touch or photograph these animals at close quarters, you may startle them and cause them to run and hurt themselves. For this reason, always keep your dogs on leads.
- **Walk quietly** through all hamlets and villages, taking care not to provoke the dogs and treating the inhabitants with courtesy.
- **Leave all gates just as you find them**, whether in the villages or in the open countryside. Although you may not see any livestock, the gates serve a purpose: they are used to keep animals in (or out of) a specific area. Here again livestock could be damaged by careless behaviour.
- **Do not pick wildflowers or other plants, or capture butterflies or invertebrates** of any sort. Not only is this prohibited in the wider countryside (and rigidly enforced in the natural parks), but you should leave them for others to enjoy.
- **Stay on the path wherever possible**. Short-cuts cause erosion and confusion, as well as damaging the surrounding vegetation.
- **Respect private property**. Contradictory as it may seem, most of these walks pass through private property, be they forests or fields. Generally speaking, however, you can wander anywhere where there isn't a fence blocking your way.
- **Take *all* your litter away with you.**

Touring

The Costa Brava and its immediate hinterland is an ideal place for car touring, offering the motorist not only a fine variety of natural sights but also an interesting selection of rural landscapes dotted with quiet villages, bustling market towns and architectural gems in the form of medieval castles and Romanesque churches.

The six car tours described here start from the main population centres of northeastern Catalonia — Barcelona, Olot, Girona and Figueres — and take in all the major habitats of the region, ranging from the rugged coast to the top of the highest peaks. These are complemented by sites of historical, architectural and archaeological interest, quiet backwaters in which to observe wildlife and a multitude of pleasant picnic spots. Each can be driven in a day — some in an afternoon — although if you attempted to visit all the sites of interest and undertake each and every short walk for motorists you could be occupied for a week!

We have deliberately avoided dual carriageways and motorways. The tours generally follow the quieter minor roads which — above all midweek — are still gloriously free of traffic. Nevertheless, many of the roads in coastal districts and popular mountain areas will be busy at weekends and in the holiday months of July and August. An important part of the region's road system is an extensive network of unsurfaced roads, used by 4WDs and normal cars alike; we have tried to avoid these, except in Car tour 5, where the unsurfaced roads are possibly in better condition than the surfaced ones!

The touring notes are brief; they include just a taste of the information available in guidebooks or leaflets from the tourist information offices. Instead we concentrate on the 'logistics' of touring — distances, road conditions and the most interesting sights — with the primary aim of showing you places to which we hope you will return to walk. Remember that most museums, information centres and such-like generally close at midday — or *all* day on Mondays — although actual opening times are variable. Only *isolated* restaurants, petrol stations and toilets are noted, as it can be assumed that any settlement described as a town will have all these facilities. Many main roads were renumbered in 2000; we have used the new numbers throughout, although other maps and signs may reflect the old system.

Traffic regulations differ little from those in the rest of Europe, but here are a few local peculiarities. Some traffic lights show flashing amber, especially in built up areas, which means that you can proceed, but with care. Many small towns split by main roads have traffic lights which turn red if you approach at more the 50kmph; local drivers often ignore them, but you should *not* follow this example under any circumstances. In towns and cities, be prepared for right turns which bring you face-to-face with a pedestrian crossing displaying the green 'walk' light. There are also far more cyclists and farm vehicles on the roads here than in most parts of Europe, which should be passed with caution and given a wide berth. Beware unpredictable weather: snow and frost in the higher stretches of Car tour 2, and sudden torrential storms and banks of fog anywhere. Valuables should *never* be left exposed in cars, especially in tourist areas near the coast. Lastly, we don't recommend that you drive immediately after a large lunch, which slows down your reflexes considerably.

The large fold-out touring map is designed to be held out opposite the touring notes. Symbols used in the text are explained in the map legend.

Take along **warm clothing, food and drink**, as you may experience delays. **Allow ample time for stops**: the estimated driving times for each tour include only short breaks at viewpoints labelled 📷 in the notes.

All motorists should read the Countryside code on page 12 and go quietly. *Bon viatge!*

Montserrat (alternative route from Mura in Car tour 1)

Tour 1: NORTH OF BARCELONA — LIMESTONE CLIFFS, WATERFALLS, ROMANESQUE CHURCHES AND RAPTORS

Barcelona • Caldes de Montbui • Sant Feliu de Codines • Sant Miquel del Fai • Sant Martí de Centelles • Centelles • Tona • Les Coves del Toll • Moià • L'Estany • Moià • Calders • Navarcles • Talamanca • Mura • Terrassa (or Montserrat) • Barcelona

172km/106.5mi; just over 4 hours' driving, for the main route. The alternative return, through Montserrat, gives a total of 212km/131.5mi and will take around 5h30min.
En route: Walks 4, 5 (Walk 3 lies on the alternative return route via Montserrat); Short walks for motorists 🚗 1, 2, 3. Barcelona is also the best base from which to access Walks 1 and 2.
On weekends there tends to be an exodus from the city to places such as

Sant Miquel del Fai, with subsequent traffic jams on the roads back into Barcelona on Sunday evenings. Beware winter fogs in low-lying areas near Tona and Navarcles.
Picnic suggestions: Sant Miquel del Fai (30km 🍴), the rich **meadow habitat** off the N141c (58km), the **Coll d'Eres** (135km; on the route of 🚗3). On the alternative return route: the narrow road alongside the **Riera de Mura** (after 126km) and **Montserrat** (165km).

The limestone mountains due north of Barcelona are renowned for their spectacular scenery, harbouring a rich flora and fauna and a wealth of historical remains and architectural gems ranging from Roman baths to pre-Romanesque churches. The later part of the main route passes through the heart of the Parc Natural de Sant Llorenç del Munt (much affected by forest fires in recent years), while the alternative finish takes you to the magnificent conglomerate pinnacles of Montserrat, where the monastery houses the small black wood-carved virgin of La Moreneta, the patron of Catalonia.

Leave **Barcelona** on the C33 motorway towards GIRONA. The kilometre readings begin as you exit the motorway at Junction 1 (just after the first toll-barrier) along the C59, signposted to SANTA PERPÈTUA DE MOGODA and CALDES DE MONTBUI. Continue north for just over 12km, then turn left into the Roman spa-town of **Caldes de Montbui ★** (13.5km *i* 🏨 ✗ 🍴 M; weekly market Tuesday morning). Follow signs to the CENTRE HISTORIC, then park and head for the Font del Lleó, a thermal spring bubbling out at a constant 70.9°C. It is opposite the recently restored Roman baths, a spa hotel and the Museu de Caldes. The tourist information point is in the museum (Tuesday-

Saturday 11.00-14.00 and 17.00-20.00; Sunday mornings). There are guided visits to the baths on Wednesdays at 12.00, Fridays at 18.00, Saturdays at 12.00 and 18.00 and Sundays at 12.00 (☎ 93 8654140; e-mail: m.caldesm@ diba.es).
Leave Caldes by heading north over the cobbles of the Passeig de Remei, to rejoin the C59 (15.5km), then continue north to **Sant Feliu de Codines** (20km 🏨 ✗ 🍴; weekly market Saturday morning). This is one of the many tranquil towns in the area that were 'discovered' by the Barcelona bourgeoisie in the 19th century and transformed by the construction of numerous weekend villas, many of dubious

15

Short walk for motorists

🚗1 Sant Miquel del Fai and Sant Martí

2km/1.25mi; 30min. An easy linear walk with no climbing, this route contours along a broad path halfway up the cliffs at Sant Miquel del Fai, passing behind the spectacular waterfalls shown below. Park behind the monastery complex (the 30km-point in the tour; see map on page 74).

From the car park head through the cleft in the cliffs down and into the monastery complex of **Sant Miquel del Fai**. Follow the only possible path alongside the cliffs, passing in front of the cave church squeezed under an overhanging cliff and then walk behind the waterfalls, where maidenhair fern and small clumps of sarcocapnos sprout from the calc tufa cliffs. The small chapel of **Sant Martí** sits on the cliff-edge (**15min**). Crag martins whiz by, and wallcreepers regularly winter here, while Bonelli's eagles and eagle owls breed elsewhere on the cliffs of the area. Below Sant Martí lies the **Cova Les Tosques** — a maze of tunnels, definitely not for the tall, claustrophobic or those suffering from vertigo. Retracing your steps to the monastery, note the path off right to the picnic site (*P⅏*) — equipped with an intriguingly named 'sun-powered log cabin bar' — and the path down to the **Cova de Sant Miquel**, another subterranean labyrinth under the cliffs. You arrive back at **Sant Miquel** after **30min**.

The tufa cliffs and waterfalls at Sant Miquel del Fai

architectural merit. Pass straight through the town, *noting the right turn to Sant Miquel del Fai 200m past the town centre*, and continue for just over 1km to **El Cim d'Àligues** (🦅). This cliff-top raptor recuperation centre organises spectacular aerial demonstrations of birds of prey. Times vary, but normally there will be flights at 12.00 midweek and at 13.00 and again at around 16.00/17.00 at weekends (☎ 93 8662648; www.get.to/cimdaligues; closed 16 Dec to 15 Jan, 1 to 15 July and Mondays throughout the year). Retrace your route back towards Sant Feliu and turn left towards SANT MIQUEL DEL FAI on the dramatic BV1485, which winds inexorably along a cliff-face towards the end of an ever-narrowing valley to reach the remarkable cave church and waterfalls of **Sant Miquel del Fai★** (30km ☀🏃🍴🎒🚗1P). Walk 5 passes through here. Park where indicated and continue on foot through a large cleft in the cliff

down to the main entrance and the recently restored group of buildings, including a still-used 10th-century church wedged under an overhanging cliff, and the obligatory restaurant (open 10.00-17.00 — later in summer; closed Mondays; (93 8658008; www. santmiqueldelfai.net).

Back at your car, follow the exit signs from the car park along a narrow road. After 350m and two hairpins, turn right at a junction signposted only RESTAURANT 3.5KM, to follow a minor unclassified road north along a river valley. You reach the C1413b east of **Sant Quirze de Safaja** (34km ✕△). Turn right here, through pleasant wooded scenery; then, at the village of **Sant Martí de Centelles** (39.5km ▮), overlooked by a ruined castle perched high on a cliff just to the north, take the track left signposted CASTELL DE SANT MARTÍ and park in the esplanade next to the church for ➾2.

Continue on the C1413b to Cen-telles (▲▲✕➾), skirting to the west of the town centre (44.5km). Then turn left (north) towards VIC on the main C17 dual carriageway (45.5km). About 4km further on, take the exit signposted TONA SUD/SEVA (49.5km), veering left under the C17. *(Or keep right to reach Seva in 5km and link up with Car tour 2.)* Almost immediately you enter unremarkable **Tona** (▲▲✕➾). Just over 1km further on, turn left uphill towards MAN-RESA on the BV5303. After about 2km bear left towards MOIÀ and COLLSUPINA on the N141c (54km) and wind quickly up into attractive wooded country. After just over 4km of bends, turn left along a minor road signposted URB. PUIGSAGORDI/CENTRE EMISSIONS, straight into perfect picnic country (**P**) — light woodland and meadows, in summer studded with clumps of blue chicory, yellow lavender-cotton and lilac-flowered *Phlomis herba-venti*. Butterflies abound in summer — Catalan furry and Damon blues,

Short walks for motorists

🚗2 Sant Martí de Centelles and the Castell de Sant Martí

2km/1.25mi; 45min; 130m/425ft ascent and descent. A quick linear botanical excursion from Sant Martí up to the ruined medieval castle perched atop a cliff just to the north of this small village. Park next to the church of Sant Martí, signposted left up a track at the 39.5km-point in the tour.

From the car park next to the church (sporting an attractive wrought-iron street lamp), take the unsurfaced road that leads behind the church (Carrer de la Font). Immediately, as you pass next to the wall enclosing the church, pick up a path heading up left into a group of mature holm oaks. Shortly you come to an area of bare, slanting rock. Ignore the path which continues straight on around the base of the rock; instead, head up to the left on another, somewhat indistinct path that takes you across the back of the exposed limestone. At the far end of the outcrop, re-enter the woods and then continue on the flat across more areas of bare rock, carpeted in spring with clumps of the strongly lemon-scented winter savory, bushes of *Ruta angusti-folia*, the tall Italian catchfly, white rock-rose, snapdragon and dipcadi (**15min**).

Once back in the woods at the end of these colourful rock gardens, wind up a disintegrating trail to a shady esplanade between two cliffs, from where you should take the roughly hewn steps up to the right. These lead to a level path around the north side of the castle (with lesser butterfly orchids and Bertoloni's ophrys en route). After about one minute, cut back up to your right along a cobbled path which takes you through an arched doorway into the centre of the ruined **Castell de Sant Martí**

(**25min**). Explore at leisure, noting fine views north and east and the abundance of ramonda on the north-facing cliff, before retracing your steps to the church in **Sant Martí** (**45min**).

🚗3 Montcau

4km/2.5mi; 1h10min; 185m/605ft ascent/descent. A there-and-back climb to the second-highest peak in the Sant Llorenç Natural Park. Park in one of the two car parks just on the south side of Coll d'Estenalles at the 135km-point in the tour. See map on page 70.

From the **Coll d'Estenalles** follow Walk 4 on page 69 to the **Coll d'Eres**, a small saddle populated with large holm oaks which provide welcome shade for a picnic (***P**; 20min*). From here cut back left up the very well-trodden path with loose stones that leads to the bare, dome-shaped peak of **Montcau** (**40min**). Retrace your steps back to **Coll d'Estenalles** (**1h10min**).

Looking up to Montcau from the narrow road to the Coll d'Eres (Short walk 3 for motorists and Walk 4)

false ilex and sloe hairstreaks, violet fritillary and chestnut heath, to name but a few.

Back on the N141c, continue left for 1km to crest the **Coll de la Pollosa** (971m/3185ft; 59km), then pass a turning to the village of Collsupina (✕). Shortly you come to a left turn (63km) marked 'Les Coves del Toll'; follow this road for 2km, until you reach the unprepossessing entrance to an interesting group of karstified caves, inhabited in Neolithic times (guided visits at weekends at 10.30 and 13.30, but on Saturdays only from April to October; midweek organised groups only). You can learn more about the caves a little further along the N141c, at the Museu Arqueològic i Paleontològic (☎ 93 8300143) in nearby **Moià** (72km *i*✝🏨🍴✕M; weekly market Sunday morning; ☎ 93 8301418 for tourist information).

In Moià, turn right at the traffic lights, back onto the C59, and drive 8km north to the delightful village of **L'Estany** (80km ✝✕M). The village name ('The Lake') refers to the lagoon, drained in 1554, that once occupied the agricultural plain to the south. The settlement lies clustered around the diminutive Romanesque Monestir de Santa Maria d'Estany, boasting a double-colonnaded cloister with remarkable capitals and a museum (open 10.00-13.00, 16.00-19.00; ☎ 93 8303139). Return to **Moià** (88km) and turn right at the traffic lights, back onto the N141c. Pass through **Calders** (98km ✕🍴) and carry on towards NAVARCLES, turning left onto the BV1221 at the PetroCat petrol station just *before* the bridge over the **river Llobregat** (107km). Within 1km, in **Navarcles** itself, look for a small sign pointing right to the MONESTIR DE SANT BENET.

To reach this jewel of Romanesque ecclesiastical architecture, follow the road across the bridge over the **Riera de Calders**, then turn right after 100m over a smaller bridge and onto a track. Bear left and park next to the sign for the **Monestir de Sant Benet** (✝).

Back in Navarcles (110km), turn right (southeast) and follow the tortuous BV1221 to the attractive medieval village of **Talamanca** (119km ✝🍴 △✕), which houses yet another delightful Romanesque church — that of Santa Maria. Some 4km further on, fork right downhill on a minor road to the village of **Mura** (126km *i*✝✕). The interesting Romanesque church of **Sant Martí**, shown on page 2, was restored in the 1980s. There are also a few rustic restaurants and a small information point for the **Parc Natural de Sant Llorenç del Munt** (open weekends only, from 10.00-14.00; ☎ 93 8318375). Return to the BV1221 *(or continue to Montserrat; see Alternative return overleaf)* for the remaining 6km to the **Coll d'Estenalles** (135km; 871m/2860ft; 🚌3 and Walk 4). Here you will find a larger park information centre, with audiovisual display (open daily from 10.00-15.00; ☎ 93 8317300).

Chestnut heath (Coenonympha glycerion)

Continue south from the Coll d'Estenalles towards the large industrial town of TERRASSA. On the outskirts, follow signs for *PARC DE VALLPARADÍS* and *ESGLÉSIES DE SANT PERE* to come into the centre of **Terrassa**★ (152km *i*✝🏛🏔M; tourist information (93 7397019). The Parc de Vall-paradís is a very well conceived park in the centre which houses three lovely churches: Sant Pere, with a stone altar (9th to 11th centuries) and a fine Romanesque mosaic; Santa Maria, home to a 5th-century mosaic and Romanesque murals; and Sant Miquel, centred around an enormous, octagonal baptismal font (closed Mondays and Sunday afternoons; (93 7833702). Also worth a visit is the Museu de la Ciència i de la Tècnica (Rambla d'Ègara, 270; (93 7368966), a museum dedicated to the development of science and technology in Catalonia (closed Mondays, afternoons in July and August and also weekend afternoons the rest of the year).

From Terrassa, pick up the C58 to return to **Barcelona** (172km).

Alternative return route via Montserrat

From **Mura** (126km) follow the narrow road west alongside the **Riera de Mura** (*P*) to **Rocafort** (131.5km ✝✕). Take the only road out of the village (BV1224), driving through light pine forest to the outskirts of **El Pont de Vilomara** (138km 🚌). Here turn right to cross the **river Llobregat** — the 'motor' of the many former textile towns which line the valley in this area — and follow signs to MANRESA along the BV1229. As you approach Manresa, *carefully* follow signs to the C55 (avoiding the C16 motorway to Barcelona, which will *not* take you to Montserrat). After 3km you cross over the busy C55, just before winding down right to join it (141km) as it heads south. Now follow signs to BARCELONA.

About 17km further on you reach **Monistrol de Montserrat** (158km ✝🏔🏠✕🚌), where you turn right along the BP1121 towards MONTSERRAT and begin a sinuous climb up towards the **Muntanya de Montserrat** itself, now towering overhead and unmistakable with its improbably sculpted skyline. After about 7km, turn left at a junction to enter the car park of the modern **Monestir de Montserrat**★ (165km *i*※✝🏔✕📷MWC*P*), which caters for the hoards of pilgrims who journey here from all over the world to pay homage to the Romanesque figurine known as La Moreneta, blackened over the centuries by candle smoke and the repeated application of varnishes. Walk 3 starts and finishes here. Return to Monistrol de Montserrat (172km) and turn right onto the C55 to return to **Barcelona** (212km).

Muntanya de Montserrat

Tour 2: EL MONTSENY — A TOUR AROUND BARCELONA'S GREEN LUNG

Sant Celoni • La Costa del Montseny • Turó de l'Home • Santa Fe • Sant Marçal • Viladrau • Espinelves • Sant Sadurní d'Osormort • Seva • El Brull • Collformic • Sant Celoni

119km/74 mi; about 3 hours' driving
En route: Walks 6, 7; Short walks
for motorists ⛟ 4, 5, 6
*Roads are good, if rather narrow in
places; the upper reaches of the road
up to Turó de l'Home is often closed
at weekends owing to the sheer
number of cars which attempt to
reach the top. Winter brings snow
and ice, both of which can hang*

*around for many weeks in sheltered
spots on north-facing slopes.*
Picnic suggestions: Les Feixes
(13km; ⛱), summit of **Turó de
l'Home** (26km), **Pantà de Santa
Fe** (36km, on the route of ⛟6),
Font de Passavets (37.5km),
banks of the **Riera Major** (after
67.5km), **Collformic** (95km)

At weekends droves of city-dwellers flock to the Montseny — barely 50km from the centre of the Barcelona conurbation — to walk, harvest wild mushrooms or simply to have lunch in one of the area's many restaurants. Yet midweek the area is an oasis of calm, and visitors will be able to enjoy a peaceful drive through the layered vegetation zones which characterise the massif. At the lowest levels you encounter umbrella pines and evergreen oaks, which blend imperceptibly with altitude into deciduous sweet chestnut, sessile oak and beech forest, also harbouring small enclaves of silver fir. From this verdant mantle emerge the bare rocky summits of Turó de l'Home (1706m/5597ft), Les Agudes (1706m/5596ft) and Matagalls (1697m/5566ft) — the highest points of the Parc Natural del Montseny.

We start in **Sant Celoni** (*i*⛽🏨🏠; market day Wednesday), a busy but otherwise unexceptional town reached from Junction 11 on the E15/A7 Barcelona/Girona motorway. Pick up the BV5114 heading north from the town centre, following signs to SANTA FE DEL MONTSENY, then turn left after 4km at a roundabout onto the BV5119 towards MOSQUEROLES. Turó de l'Home, its beech forests tinged orange in autumn, rises in the distance to your right, its summit fully 1.5km above you! The road quickly abandons the fertile plains of the Montseny foothills to enter thick woodland. First you come to cork oaks, their stripped trunks standing out bright red, then umbrella pines,

commercially exploited for their pine kernels. Soon you pass below the small village of **Mosqueroles** (6km ✖) and arrive 5km further on at a junction (11km), where you turn right. *(The tour returns to this junction after another 100km.)* Within 300m turn right again, down into the hamlet of **La Costa del Montseny** (*i*⛽✖), equipped with one of the Montseny's many information centres (December-February open 11.00-14.00 at weekends only; the rest of the year open daily and until 17.30 at weekends). Rejoin the road at the far end of La Costa, continuing uphill to the excellent picnic spot of **Les Feixes** (13km ⛱PWC) on your left, then on to an information point and car park at the **Coll**

Short walks for motorists

🚗4 Les Agudes

3km/1.9mi; 50min; 98m/320ft of ascent/descent. A linear walk along the highest and most spectacular ridge in the Montseny, following part of Walk 6 in the opposite direction (map page 77). Park at the 26km-point in the tour.

From wherever you are obliged to park on the road up to **Turó de l'Home** (photograph overleaf), continue on foot as far as **Coll Sesbasses**, the saddle which takes you from the southwest side of the ridge over to the northeast face. From here a path, marked by green metal posts with blue squares (indicating the GR-5/2), heads north along the east side of the ridge all the way to the **Coll de les Agudes**, a grassy saddle at the base of the rocky peak. Climb to the summit of **Les Agudes** (**30min**) for spectacular views, then retrace your steps to **Coll Sesbasses** (**50min**).

🚗5 Pantà de Santa Fe

4km/2.5mi; 1h; 45m/150ft of descent/ascent. A circular walk down from the Can Casades information point to the Pantà de Santa Fe, a small reservoir ringed by beech woods and an ideal picnic spot. Park outside Can Casades, the 36km-point in the tour. See map on page 77.

From the information point at **Can Casades** head northeast down the unsurfaced road towards the Hotel Santa Fe, turning right in 100m/yds down a track signposted 'Pantà de Santa Fe'. After four minutes, ignore a track off left next to a huge, rounded granite boulder. Instead follow the track downhill through the beech forest and then keep left at a T-junction (**15min**), down to the shores of the reservoir (**P**; **20min**), an ideal picnic spot. Continue southeast as far as the broad track which crosses the dam (**25min**); once across, turn left

(now following green posts with orange stickers) on a track which first follows the northern shore of the *pantà* and then the banks of the **Riera de Santa Fe** (photograph page 25) — haunt of fire salamander and golden-ringed dragonfly — back uphill towards the hotel. After **55min**, turn left to cross the *riera* on a couple of small wooden bridges, then negotiate a set of stairs to return to the Hotel and the unsurfaced road back to **Can Casades** (**1h**).

Pheasant's-eye daffodils (Narcissus poeticus) on the slopes of Les Agudes; bottom: Les Agudes, with Avetosa in the foreground (see also Walk 6)

de la Plana and **Font Martina** (15km *i*🚙).

From here on the road narrows considerably, after 4km entering the first of the beech forests which clothe most of the upper slopes of the Montseny. At the next junction (20km), the road up to the left will take you all the way to the summit of **Turó de l'Home** (26km ✳🗙🚙4*P* and Walk 6), although because of the limited space available, you may be obliged to park some way before the top (generally on fine weekends) and walk the last stretch.

Return to the summit junction (32km) and continue left through mature beech forests, turning left on the BV5114 (35km) to reach the cluster of hotels and restaurants known as **Santa Fe de Montseny** (36km ✳*i*▲🗙🗚WC 🚌5). Here you'll find the natural park information point of **Can Casades** (open daily from 10.00-15.00 and 16.00-19.00; ℂ 93 8475113). Walk 6 starts here.

Continue north on the BV5114, past the car park at **Font de Passavets** (37.5km ♪ *P*; en route in Walk 6), to be regaled with magnificent views of the Pyrenees to the north, the coast away to the east and, towering up to your left, the sheer northern slopes of **Les Agudes**.

Continuing north, stop awhile at the pass of **Sant Marçal** (44km ✳✝▲🗙🗃), which separates the massifs of Les Agudes/Turó de l'Home and Matagalls, where the eponymous monastery has been converted into a luxury hotel. To the right of the road here lies the **Taula dels Tres Bisbes**, a modern representation in stone of the table and chairs used by the bishops of Barcelona, Girona and Vic who, tradition has it, used to sit here at the confluence of their respective dioceses to discuss ecclesiastical affairs.

From Sant Marçal onwards, the road descends quickly, leaving the

Short walk for motorists

🚐6 Puig Ventós
6km/3.75mi; 1h30min; 90m/295ft of ascent/descent. This linear route gives you a quick look at the rolling plateau of La Calma, much the lowest and the 'poor relation' of the three main massifs of the Montseny. Park at Collformic, the 95km-point in the tour, and use the map on page 82.

From **Collformic**, pick up the track signposted 'El Pla de la Calma' that runs roughly southwards *above* the restaurant towards the long flat ridge of La Calma. As you reach the main ridge of **La Calma** (**30min**), turn left at a saddle and head east along a grassy ridge which soon starts to become rather rocky. This leads to the summit of **Puig Ventós** (Windy Peak; **50min**), with fine views east to the heights of Matagalls, Les Agudes and Turó de l'Home. Retrace your steps to **Collformic** (**1h30min**).

Above: Turó de l'Home in winter; below: summer-flowering French lavender (Lavandula stoechas)

beech forest behind and entering solid masses of holm oak. At the junction with the GI543 (51km), turn left to detour to **Viladrau** (53.5km 🏘🏠✕), a village of Virginia creeper-bedecked villas, highly fashionable with the Catalan bourgeoisie in centuries past as a summer resort. Back at the junction of the GI543 and BV5114 (56km), continue straight on to another junction (59km), where you turn left along the GI544, shortly passing under the C25 trunk road (which will play hide-and-seek with us for several kilometres). **Espinelves** (61km 🚻🏘△✕) is much less pretentious than Viladrau and is renowned primarily for the elegant 12th-century Romanesque church of Sant Vicenç d'Espinelves, topped off with an imposing three-storey bell-tower. Aside from the church, Espinelves is also well known for the Fira de l'Avet, an outdoor Christmas tree-market which takes place each year during the first week of December. Continuing on past Espinelves, still on the GI544, turn right at a roundabout (66.5km) along the BV5201 to **Sant Sadurní d'Osormort** (67.5km 🚻△✕*P*). This one-horse hamlet, where the 12th-century Romanesque church has suffered a rather botched restoration, boasts a wonderful picnic spot next to the river. To get there, continue along the road past the church for 100m and then walk left past the white-painted Refugi de Pescadors and down a flight of steps to a footbridge over the **Riera Major**.

Return to the roundabout outside Sant Sadurní (68.5km) and turn right on the BV5201 towards SANT JULIÀ DE VILATORTA. Then, at a house called La Fullaca (71km), go left under the C25 towards VILADRAU on the BV5251. After 6km turn right on the B520,

Above: the Taula dels Tres Bisbes; left: the Riera de Santa Fe (Short walk 5 for motorists); below left: the red sandstone buildings of El Brull, with the church of Sant Martí

point (10.00-14.30 and 15.00-18.00; closed Tuesdays and Wednesdays in winter; (93 8840692). From here the road meanders up through steep holm oak forests to **Collformic** (1145m/3755ft; 95km ❄✖️🎦 🚐6*P*), a very popular weekend destination for serious ramblers, strollers and gastronomes alike. Walk 7 starts here.

Follow the road southwards as it zigzags tightly down to the small village of **Montseny** (107km ▲△✖️🚐), the whole route amply furnished with rustic restaurants catering for hungry Barcelonans and motorists. Continuing on the BV5301 below Montseny, turn left after 1km along a narrow road signposted LA COSTA, which takes you out onto the BV5119 just below La Costa (11km on your outgoing route; now 111km). Turn right here to return to **Sant Celoni** (119km).

following signposting to 'VIC 17' (77km). Some 2.5km further on turn left on the BV5303 towards SEVA.

Once in **Seva** (85.5km ✝▲✖️🚐), another village of second homes, turn left on the BV5031. *(Or keep straight on to reach **Tona** in 5km, if you want to link up with Car tour 1.)* You climb quickly to the small hamlet of **El Brull** (89km *i*✝✖️), built out of the local red sandstone and harbouring the eye-catching 11th-century Roman-esque church of Sant Martí, two restaurants and a park information

Tour 3: LA GARROTXA AND EL PLA DE L'ESTANY — VOLCANOES, MEDIEVAL VILLAGES AND LAKES

Olot • *Fageda d'en Jordà* • *Volcà del Croscat* • *Santa Pau* • El Torn • Les Estunes • *Estany de Banyoles* • *Porqueres* • *Serinyà* • *Besalú* • Castellfollit de la Roca • Olot

73km/45.5mi, two hours' driving
En route: Walks (8-10), 11, 12;
Short walks for motorists 🚗 7, 8, 9, 10
Note: a bypass around Besalú is due to open during 2007, so access details may vary from those given in the text.

Picnic suggestions: Parc Nou in Olot, Santa Pau (8.5km), river Ser at El Torn (21.5km), Les Estunes (35km), beside the Estany de Banyoles (after 36km), La Resclosa de Serinyà (after 48km; on the route of 🚗10)

This tour first visits the *comarca* of La Garrotxa, renowned for its extensive volcanic landscape encompassing thickly wooded lava flows and 40 dormant volcanoes. Then we move on to the *comarca* of El Pla de l'Estany and the Estany de Banyoles, the second largest permanent lake in the Iberian Peninsula. The minor roads of the first half of the tour in part follow the route of the original cart-track that linked Olot and Banyoles in the Middle Ages, passing through the natural splendours of the Parc Natural de la Zona Volcànica de La Garrotxa (PNZVG). The return along the Girona-Olot trunk road takes in the splendid medieval towns of Besalú and Castellfollit de la Roca.

Our starting point is the relaxed market town of Olot★ (✳*i*🛏 ⛺🏠 △✳M; Monday morning market), the capital of the *comarca* of La Garrotxa. (Walks 8-12 are easily accessible from here.) Completely rebuilt after the destruction wreaked by the earthquakes of 1427 and 1428, today Olot is a curious mix of Renaissance, Baroque and Art Nouveau buildings (information from the tourist office, C/ Bisbe Lorenzana 15; ☎ 972 260141; e-mail: turisme@olot.org). The town boasts two important museums: the Museu Comarcal de la Garrotxa (C/de l'Hospici, 8; closed Tuesday and Sunday afternoons; ☎ 972 279130), with a fine collection of paintings from the 19th-century Olot school of landscape artists, and the Museu Parroquial de Sant Esteve, known principally for its El Greco (housed in the Església de Sant Esteve; visits during mass or by prior arrange-

ment; ☎ 972 260474).
Also located within Olot are the Montsacopa volcano — an ideal place for an evening stroll — and El Casal/Museu dels Volcans, which doubles as an interpretation centre for the *parc natural* and provides an excellent insight into the complex subject of vulcanology (open July and August from 10.00-14.00 and 17.00-19.00; closed Sunday afternoons; open September to June from 10.00-14.00 and 18.00-20.00; closed Tuesdays and Sunday afternoons; ☎ 972 266762). The museum is set in the heart of the well-landscaped Parc Nou botanical gardens (✳✳*P*), where Walk 11 starts and finishes.
The km readings begin at the BP garage on the southern outskirts of Olot, at the roundabout at the junction of Carretera de Santa Pau and Avinguda de Sant Jordi. Pick up the GI524 heading southeast towards SANTA PAU. Despite

Short walks for motorists

🚶7 La Fageda d'en Jordà
1.5km/1mi; 25min. An all-but-level, lollipop-shaped route that takes you into the heart of the renowned beech forest of d'en Jordà. This is walk 2 of the PNZVG and is signposted in sky-blue. Park at the PNZVG informa-tion point of Can Serra, the 3.5km-point in the tour. See map page 95.
Leave **Can Serra** as for Walk 12 (page 98), but at the first sign turn right along SENDER JOAN MARA-GALL, a path named after the poet who inimitably described those who walk through the Fageda as 'prisoners to its silence and ver-dancy'. The path, following posts with blue diamonds, takes you to the base of a large *tossol* (**10min**). These characteristic hemispherical protuberances (up to 20m/65ft high) were formed in the lava flows as trapped bubbles of gas escaped. The path circumnavigates the *tossol*, after which you follow your outward route back to **Can Serra** (**25min**).

🚶8 El Volcà del Croscat
3km/1.9mi; 40min; minimal climb-ing. A short, almost circular stroll following PNZVG walk 15 to the information point of Can Passavent, from where you can visit the colourful exposed innards of Croscat — the peninsula's largest volcano. Park at the Àrea de Santa Margarida, the 6km-point in the tour. Map page 98.
From the **Àrea de Santa Marga-rida**, follow the notes for Walk 12

on page 100 to **Can Passavent** (**20min**) and into the heart of the *greders* — an old quarry. Until it was closed in 1991, it had eaten away a slice of the volcano from the top of its cone to the base, thereby exposing 100m/330ft-high cliffs of volcanic ash and detritus. After the circular tour of the quarry, return to **Can Passa-vent** (**30min**), then head east as in Walk 12. But on meeting the road, turn *right* to return to the **Àrea de Santa Margarida** (**40min**).

🚶9 El Volcà de Santa Margarida
3km/1.9mi; 1h05min; 180m/590ft of ascent/descent. A linear walk up and into the well-preserved volcano of Santa Margarida, following a section of Walk 12 in the reverse direction. Park us for Short walk 8 above. See map on page 98.
Starting from the **Àrea de Santa Margarida**, head southwest uphill along a track following signs to SANTA MARGARIDA. At a crossroads in the midst of a pine plantation (about **5min**), turn right uphill. Pass through the farmyard of **Can Caselles**, bearing left to continue uphill towards some enormous sweet chestnut trees, then curve right up a steep section of track. This takes you to the lip of the **Volcà de Santa Margarida** (**30min**). At this point, turn right along the track which follows the lip and, on reaching a turreted house on your left (Can Santa), turn left down into the heart of the crater (**35min**). In the centre of the open floor of the crater stands the small chapel of **Santa Marga-rida**, originally Romanesque but substantially rebuilt after the earthquakes of the 15th century. Retrace your steps to the **Àrea de Santa Margarida** (**1h05min**).

The greders *of El Volcà del Croscat*

27

Olot's increasingly sprawling suburbs, you quickly enter a pleasant rural landscape, where small farms relieve the monotony of the thick oak and beech woods. A succession of excellent restaurants occupies this first stretch: a fine *paella* can be enjoyed in l'Hostal de l'Arç (✕ on the left after 1km), with grilled lamb a speciality of l'Hostal dels Ossos (✕ 1km or so further on).

Soon you reach the car park and PNZVG information point at **Can Serra** (3.5km *i*WC🚗7; see map on page 98), from which you can explore the famous lowland beech forest of **Fageda d'en Jordà** (❋), which today cloaks the lava flow that spewed out from the volcano of **El Croscat** some 11,500 years ago. Walk 12 starts here, while the short option of Walk 11 also passes through.

Continue east past the restaurant at **Can Xel** (5km ✕), and shortly come to the large car park known as the **Àrea de Santa Margarida** (6km WC🚗8, 9), through which Walk 12 passes. A little further on you reach the splendidly preserved medieval village of **Santa Pau★** (8.5km *i*✝🛍🛏△✕🚗*P*), with the Serra de Finestres (Walk 8) as a magnificent backdrop. Turn right towards the old village where signposted, park immediately, then follow the pedestrian walkways into the medieval centre. Like Olot, this part of the town was rebuilt after the earthquakes of the 15th century. Today it possesses

an attractive harmony of architectural styles, including the imposingly 'square' Castell de Sant Pau and the pair of arched, triangular squares known as La Placeta dels Balls and El Firal dels Bous.

From Santa Pau continue east through pleasant farmland and forest, passing through the hamlet of **El Sallent** (12.5km). When you reach a road junction on the outskirts of sleepy **Mieres** (17.5km ✝✕), turn left towards EL TORN 4KM on the GIV5243. Park by the church at the entrance to the hamlet of **El Torn** (21.5km ✝*P*) and walk down to the left towards the **river Ser**. Follow the river upstream for a myriad of picnic opportunities amid clouds of butterflies — Spanish festoon, southern white admiral and false ilex hairstreak, to name but three — and damselflies such as *Calopteryx xanthostoma* (similar to the banded demoiselle) and *Platycnemis latipes*.

Return from El Torn towards Mieres, but turn off left after less than 1km, to **El Santuari de Santa Maria del Colell** (23km ✝), an enormous and uninteresting building used as a retreat. Far more pleasing architecturally are the delightful, perfectly arched medieval bridge of **Pont de Can Prat★**, apparently leading nowhere in particular, which you come across on your left (27km), and then the splendid Romanesque church of **Sant Miquel de Campmajor** (✝), signposted right just 500m/yds further on. Continuing south along this road, you rejoin the GI524 from Olot (29km), where you should turn left towards BANYOLES.

Just after passing the village sign

for Porqueres, turn right to the car park for **Les Estunes** (35km ✳*P*). The surface of this small, well-wooded outcrop of calc tufa (a 'spongy' rock formed by the deposition of calcium carbonate from lime-rich waters) has been rent by intriguing crevasses during past seismic movements.

From here the road leads you into a one-way system in the suburbs of the rather disappointing town of **Banyoles★** (36km *i*🚶 ⛰⛰ ⛺ △M). Turn left at the first set of traffic lights, then take the second left, signposted to L'ESGLÉSIA DE PORQUERES, along the shores of the **Estany de Banyoles** (✳📷*P*). This substantial lake — approximately 2100m by 750m, with a maximum depth of 130m — is fed by subterranean water originating

Pont de Can Prat

Short walk for motorists

🚗10 La Resclosa de Serinyà
*4km/2.5mi; 1h; 60m/195ft of descent/ascent. A woodland stroll down to a dammed stretch of the river Fluvià — an idyllic picnic spot and an excellent place to observe herons, ducks, kingfisher, lesser spotted woodpecker, golden oriole and otters. Park near the 48km-point in the tour: just as an uphill three-lane section of the road ends, turn sharp right along a track signposted 'Camí d'Esponellà' and 'La Central 2.2km'. If there is room, park immediately; if not, continue along the track until you find a space (**do not block track entrances**).*

Assuming you have parked near the road, continue east along the track between fields and then woodland, bear right at a fork and continue to where the track splits again (**15min**). Follow the right-hand fork downhill past an attractively restored house just above you to your left, then pass a second desirable country residence just as the track begins to descend more steeply. After a final hairpin bend, you reach a semi-sunken bridge over the **river Ser**, which you cross to continue on to **La Resclosa de Serinyà** — the confluence of the Ser and the **river Fluvià** (**30min**). The Fluvià is dammed 500m/yds further downstream. From here, retrace your steps back up the hill to your vehicle (**1h**).

in the mountains of the Alta Garrotxa (the series of impressive crags visible to the north of the road between Olot and Besalú) which upwells into the *estany* through a massive underwater fault. Although too deep to be of much interest for birds, it is noted for its diverse community of damselflies and dragonflies (including robust lesser emperors and scarce chasers), especially on its western shores.

As you follow the margin of the Estany, you skirt the small satellite lagoon of **Estanyol del Vilar** (40km ✳) then, within 500m, you suddenly reach the beautiful 12th-century church of Santa Maria de **Porqueres** (👣△✖), with its arresting façade of progressively receding horseshoe arches. Inside the church, a one-euro coin gets you lights and Bach!

About 1km further north, just after you cross the **Riera Castellana**, you can pull over as signposted and take a stroll left to **Estanyol Gran** (✳) — another of the ten satellite lakes which dot the plain around Banyoles. At the next junction (42.5km), you could turn right to the 'Zona de Bany' swimming area, 1.5km distant. But the main tour turns left along the C150a, the old Banyoles/Olot road, then over and abruptly down onto the busy C66 (45km). After less than 1km you come to **Les Coves del Reclau** (✳M) on your right — a series of very visitable caves used by Palaeolithic hunter-gathers up to 200,000 years ago (open daily from 11.00-19.00 July-September, but closed Mondays for the rest of year; ✆ 972 593310).

Once through **Serinyà** (✖🚗), the next village, just at the end of an uphill stretch of three-lane road, a track off to the right

Swallowtail
(Papilio machaon)

Besalú

signposted CAMI D'ESPONELLÀ and LA CENTRAL 2.2KM (48km) leads down to the **Resclosa de Serinyà** for 🚗10(*P*). Continue on to **Besalú★** (52km ☀*i*🛈🏔🏔△✕ 🛒🅿️), one of medieval Catalonia's most important towns and once capital of El Comtat de Besalú, a small but independent earldom from 894 until it became part of the House of Barcelona in 1111. Park just before the bridges over the **river Fluvià**. Today Besalú still boasts a fine selection of medieval civil and religious architecture including, surely, the most photographed bridge in Catalonia — complete with gatehouse and kink in the middle — and a *miqwe* (a very well-preserved Romanesque Jewish bath-house). Continuing along the C66, bypass unremarkable **Argelaguer** (57km ✕) and then skirt Sant Jaume de Llierca (60km ✕). Some 2km further on, where the dual carriageway heads off directly to Olot, bear right to **Castellfollit de la Roca★** (☀🛈🏔 ✕🅿️M). This medieval settlement is instantly recognisable by its position, perched foursquare on sheer basalt cliffs at the tail end of an exposed lava flow, 60m/200ft above the river Fluvià. The best way to visit

Castellfollit is to turn left at the small green sign on the right indicating BARRI DEL FLUVIÀ, 200m/yds before the road crosses the river. After negotiating a hairpin bend, drive 500m further, then park next to an undulating wooden footbridge over the river. From here a path climbs up through tidy allotments, separated by walls of volcanic rock, into the picturesque old town.

Returning to the main road, cross the river Fluvià, and wind up the lava flow into modern **Castellfollit** (65km), where the principal attraction is the Museu de l'Embotit, dedicated to the intricacies of the sausage-making process!

From Castellfollit, continue towards Olot, rejoining the new road and taking the turn off to OLOT/LES TRIES (approximately 72km), to regain the centre of **Olot** (73km).

Tour 4: THE BAIX EMPORDÀ: MEDIEVAL VILLAGES, WILD SHORES AND CORK OAK FORESTS

Girona • Púbol • Madremanya • Monells • Cruïlles • La Bisbal d'Empordà • Peratallada • Ruïnes d'Ullastret • Torroella de Montgrí • L'Estartit • Torroella de Montgrí • Platja de Pals • Pals • Begur • Sa Tuna • Begur • Tamariu • Llafranc • Calella de Palafrugell • Cap Roig • Palafrugell • Platja del Castell • Palamós • Sant Feliu de Guíxols • Sant Grau • Llagostera • Girona

220km/136mi; 5-6 hours' driving (a more relaxed two-day tour may be a better option).
En route: Walks (8), 13, 14, 15, 16; Short walks for motorists 🚗 11, 12, 13, 14. (Walk 8 is easily reached from Girona.)
Roads are all good, if rather tortuous on the last section, and can be

extremely busy at weekends in the spring and summer.
Picnic suggestions: Ruïnes d'Ullastret (41.5km), **Platja de Pals** (about 70km), **Tamariu** (108km), **Far de Sant Sebastià** (112km), **Platja del Castell** (133km), **Puig de les Cadiretes** (179.5km, on the route of 🚗14)

This tour of the *comarca* of Baix (lower) Empordà explores the medieval villages of the coastal hinterland as well as providing an insight into the two faces of the Costa Brava: on the one hand, the cork oak-clad mountains of the Cadiretes and some of the few remaining unspoilt coves and beaches of the central Costa Brava and, on the other, a glimpse of the sprawl of skyscraper tourist hotels in Platja d'Aro.

The tour starts in **Girona★** (*i✝🏔▲🚠M🚗*11), an extremely welcoming city with a magnificently preserved old central district *(casc antic)*, complete with Jewish quarter and museum (open daily 10.00-18.00; on Sundays closes at 15.00; from June-October closes at 20.00; ✆ 972 216761; fax: 972 214618; e-mail: callgirona@ ajgirona.org. There is also a majestic Romanesque/Gothic cathedral. This fascinating building comprises a single Gothic nave — the widest in Europe — which rather dwarfs the attached Romanesque bell-tower (known as La Torre de Carlemany) and the trapezoidal cloister; it also contains an alabaster altar, an 11th-century bishop's throne carved from a single block of marble, and a renowned 12th-century tapestry depicting scenes from the Creation.
From Girona head north to pick up the C66 towards PALAMÓS.

Our km readings begin at the Repsol petrol station on the outskirts of the village of **Celrà** (about 10km from the centre of Girona). Once through **Bordils** and past **Flaçà**, turn right (10km) along the GIV6425 towards LA PERA and PÚBOL. Skirt round La Pera and, at a junction (12km), go straight on to **Púbol★** (✗M), which was once home to Salvador Dalí and his wife Gala. Today the Casa-Museu Castell Gala Dalí — which Dalí restored as a present for Gala — can be visited from March 15th to November 1st (not Mondays, except between June 15th and September 15th; ✆ 972 488655; Fax 972 488653; e-mail: pbgrups@dali-estate.org). Retrace your route towards La Pera and shortly turn left to **Pedrinyà** (15km), continuing through fields of drowsy sunflowers to **Madremanya** (18km ✝✗), the first of three delightfully preserved medieval

Short walk for motorists

🚗11 La Vall de Sant Daniel
*3km/1.9mi; 1h; 100m/330ft of
ascent/descent. A circular route
around the surprisingly rural
outskirts of Girona, along the
charming Vall de Sant Daniel and
climbing the pine-clad Muntanya de
la O. Park anywhere in Girona and
head for the cathedral steps.*

At the bottom of the massive
flight of steps that leads up to the
main entrance of **Girona
Cathedral**, head north downhill
through an archway, carrying
straight on at a crossroads to a
small square. From here, head
right along the cobbled CARRER
DELS GALLIGANTS and pass between
the 12th-century Església de Sant
Nicolau and the Museu
Arqueològic (open 10.00-14.00
and 16.00-18.00; closed Mondays
and Sunday afternoons), the latter
housed in the octagonal-towered
**Monestir de Sant Pere de
Galligants** (**5min**).

Carry on uphill along the cobbled
street, continuing in the same
direction once the cobbles end and
the CARRER DE SANT DANIEL begins.
A small stream accompanies you
on the right and after about five
minutes, the **Font del Bisbe**, half-
hidden over a small bridge on the
other side of the stream, provides
good fresh water in all but the
driest periods. Continuing along
the Carrer de Sant Daniel, the
walls to your left now hide the
still-occupied Benedictine
Monestir de Sant Daniel. Then,
as the road crosses the stream, you
suddenly enter a more rural
environment with nightingale,
Sardinian warbler, tree sparrow,
serin and cirl bunting all calling
from the hedgerows in spring.
Presently, on reaching a fork
where a road and a track enter
from the right on either side of a
tributary stream, turn right along
the track which runs on the *near*

side of the stream, continuing
almost immediately uphill to the
right, away from the stream and
along the edge of a field. Then cut
off sharp right into the courtyard
of a ruined farm (**25min**).
Heading sharply up to your left
from in front of the farm, you
encounter a narrow red-earth,
almost gully-like path which
ascends steeply into the pinewoods
of the **Muntanya de la O**. Turn
left on the cross-path you meet at
the top of the climb to a grassy
plateau with a small CHAPEL in its
midst and then continue straight
on towards the distant telecom-
munications tower, quickly
coming to a bigger track just
beneath a power line. Cross
directly over the track onto a small
path heading up the hillside (look
out for dull ophrys and giant
orchids in the scrub here in early
spring), to reach a children's
playground, bus shelter and a
junction of five streets on the TOP
OF THE RIDGE (**35min**).
Of the three streets which head
more or less northwest from here,
choose the left-hand (unnamed)
one heading downhill between
houses on the right and small
market gardens on the left.
Continue straight on as the asphalt
turns to concrete, then cross
straight over another track onto a
path. Descend to the left of a
pylon, to meet a street. Turn right
here to reach the CITY WALLS and a
METAL FOOTBRIDGE (**45min**).
For the best of the old town, head
under the footbridge, passing the
façade of the new university on
your right, and continue down
into the **Plaça de Sant Domènec**.
From here drop downhill at
random through the maze of
alleys, courtyards and narrow
flights of steps of the old Jewish
Quarter to reach **Girona
Cathedral** once more (**1h**).

villages explored in the tour. At the entrance to Madremanya, turn left and then left again 100m further on, taking the GIV6701 to **Monells** (22.5km ✝✗) — the second of the trio. Here, turn right just beyond the last house in the village (signposted ARCS DE MONELLS), cross a bridge over the normally dry stream and, opposite Restaurant Monells (23.5km), turn left to **Cruïlles** (26km ✝◾✗), the last of the three. Once in this village, park near the chemist *(farmàcia)* to explore on foot. Then drive another 100m through the village and bear right at a fork, to the somewhat worse-for-wear Romanesque church of Sant Miquel de Cruïlles (26.5km), which once formed part of a larger monastery complex of the same name, obvious on the hillside ahead. Back in Cruïlles, bear right downhill to pick up the GI644 and turn left towards LA BISBAL, where you rejoin the C66.

La Bisbal d'Empordà★ (30.5km

Cap de la Barra (Short walk 12 for motorists)

i✝⛪🏔🏔M; tourist information
(972 645166; weekly market
Friday morning) is the capital of
the Baix Empordà and an
important centre for the
manufacture and sale of pottery
and ceramics of all shapes and
sizes; Walk 13 starts and finishes
here. At the set of traffic lights on
the main road through La Bisbal
from Girona, turn left for the
pottery shops; otherwise turn
right and head through the town
centre (containing a fine
Romanesque castle/palace, once
home to the bishops of Girona;
closed Mondays and Sunday
afternoons) towards the coast.
Then turn left on the GI644
(31.5km) signposted towards
ULLASTRET and PERATALLADA. On
your left here you will see the
village of **Vulpellac** (✝⛪✗); the
entrance is on the left 200m past
the road junction. It is notable for
its Gothic-Renaissance Castell-
Palau (stately home). On reaching
a fork (34km), bear right on the
GI651 to visit the delightfully
restored village of **Peratallada**
(36km ✝⛪✗), partly surrounded
by natural rock walls and clustered
around the splendid square tower
of its castle.
Return to the GI644 (38km) and
turn right towards ULLASTRET on a
straight road heading directly
towards the mountains of
Montgrí, passing **Ullastret**
(41km) and then turning right
500m further on to the **Ruïnes
d'Ullastret★** (🍴📷wc**M***P*), an
excavated Iberian settlement
dating from the 6th century BC
(open 10.00 daily except
Mondays; (972 179058).
Back on the GI644 (43km),
continue north to **Serra de Daró**
(45.5km ✗🍴), where you turn
right on the GI643 towards
TORROELLA, reaching a large
roundabout some 5km further on
(50km). Turn left here on the

Short walk for motorists

🚗12 La Calella
*2.5km/1.5mi; 1h. You follow a
sender local which heads north
from L'Estartit to a rocky cove in a
miniature, linear version of Walk
16 (see map on page 111 and
photograph opposite). This short
walk encompasses two 85m/280ft
climbs and descents. Take
swimwear. Park anywhere in
L'Estartit (57km in the tour) and
walk towards the harbour at the
eastern edge of the town to find the
first sign.*
Opposite the **L'Estartit
harbour,** head up CARRER DEL
CAP DE LA BARRA following the
sender local signs to 'Cala Calella
22min'. Ignore a first left turn
(Carrer dels Pins) just before you
hairpin left. Carry on to the end
of the road, where a sign points
you up a flight of steps and takes
you to a scrubby HILLTOP
(**10min**), decorated in spring
with similar flowers to those
described for Walk 16. Here,
take the right-hand path (note
the green and white waymarks
on a tree), which shortly brings
you to the cliff-top; the vertical
precipice of **Cap de la Barra** is
just 20m/yds to your right
(frequented by alpine and pallid
swifts in spring and summer).
Continue northwards on the
path to Cala Calella; just after
ignoring a path off to the right,
drop down through the pines to
reach the dramatic craggy inlet
of **Els Arquets** and then, just a
little further on, descend further
to the small rocky cove of **La
Calella** (**30min**). Return along
the same route to **L'Estartit**
(**1h**).

Sant Miquel de Cruïlles (top) and the small resort of Sa Tuna

never-completed shell of the 13th-century Castell de Montgrí, which is visited during Walk 15.

From Torroella, continue on the GI641 to **L'Estartit** (57km *i*🏔🛌🏕⚠✕🚌12; weekly market Thursday) — essentially a tourist resort and marina — but with splendid if busy beaches to the south, excellent scuba-diving possibilities and trips in glass-bottomed boats around the **Illes Medes**, a nearby group of islets which is a *reserva marina*. The tourist office is situated at the port (open daily from 09.00-21.00, except lunch times and Sunday afternoons; ☎ 972 751910). Walk 16 starts and finishes in L'Estartit. Retrace your route back through **Torroella** to the roundabout reached after 50km (now 64km) and head south towards PALS along the C31. For an interesting mixture of beach and wetland habitats, including rice paddies, visit the **Gola del Ter** (mouth of the **river Ter**; ✳) and the **Platja de Pals** (⚠✕✳P): turn left 400m past the roundabout and follow the tarmac until it ends after about 6km next to the restaurant Ter-Mar. Head for the relatively quiet beach and explore the river mouth for migrant waders, the reed-beds for night herons and egrets from the breeding colony on the Illes Medes, which come here to feed, and the relict dune systems for yellow horned-poppy, tragacanth and early spider ophrys, plus reptiles such as three-toed skink, spiny-footed lizard and both large and Spanish psammodromus. Back on the C31 (77km), continue to another large round-about (84km) where you turn right for a 500m detour to the rather twee medieval walled village of **Pals★** (*i*🏔🛌🏕⚠✕🚉📷), popular with coach parties but,

C31, immediately crossing the **river Ter** and entering **Torroella de Montgrí** (51km ⛳🛌🏔⚠△ ✕M; weekly market Monday), an important royal town in the Middle Ages and one which, like so many of the main settlements in the area, was established well inland for fear of attack by the many Moorish pirates that once roamed the Mediterranean. Walk 15 starts and ends here. Visit the interesting Museu de Torroella (C/Major 31; open from 10.00 but closed Tuesdays and Sundays; ☎ 972 757301), the fine arched Plaça Major and the church of Sant Genís. Torroella is also home to a renowned international music festival in July/August each year. To the north of the town looms the Muntanya de Santa Caterina (308m/1010ft), topped off by the

nevertheless, boasting excellent views over the Baix Empordà plain. Park in the new town to stroll up to the perfectly restored old quarter.

Returning to the roundabout (85km), take the GI653 via **Regencós** (✕) to visit **Begur** (92km *i♿🏨⚓▲△✕🅿🖼M*; tourist information (972 624520; weekly market Wednesday morning), yet another Costa Brava settlement located a few prudent kilometres inland. As you approach the centre of Begur, follow signs towards SA TUNA, skirting the town to the north, and park in a public car park; from here you can explore the narrow streets of the old town, dominated by the Castell de Begur, dating from the 11th century. Continue along the same road from the car park down to **Sa Tuna** (96km), one of the most select of the many small, relatively peaceful coves along this exceedingly rugged shore. From here you can walk south along the coast as far as Punta des Plom.

Returning to **Begur** (100km), head back towards PALS on the GI653. But at a roundabout 200m after leaving Begur, turn left on the GIP6531 towards FORNELLS and AIGUABLAVA. Under 2km further on turn left again down towards another exclusive stretch of coast. FORNELLS (⚓✕), with its small beach, is signposted left after about 2.5km (a detour of 2km there and back), but perhaps TAMARIU is the better option: to reach it, fork right 800m beyond the turn-off to Fornells, then negotiate numerous curves until you drop down into **Tamariu** (108km ⚓△✕*P*). Walk 14 passes through this most pleasant of resorts, along what is without a doubt the least-spoilt stretch of the central Costa Brava.

Leave Tamariu along the

GIV6542 towards PALAFRUGELL, turning left where signposted (110.5km) to the **Far de Sant Sebastià** (112km ⚓✕🖼wc*P*), a modern lighthouse, also visited during Walk 14, which boasts fine views along the rugged coast to the south.

From here drop down quickly along PASSEIG DE PAU CASALS towards the relaxed twin resorts of CALELLA DE PALAFRUGELL and LLAFRANC. About 1.5km beyond the lighthouse, pass through a narrow gap between two pines to a convenient car park (113.5km), from which you can wander down to the beach at **Llafranc** (⚓▲△ ✕), then continue to Calella by keeping straight on through the car park following the TOTES DIRECCIONS sign until you reach sea level, where you head straight along behind the beach, turning sharply right after 500m towards PALAFRUGELL and CALELLA DE PALAFRUGELL. After a further 500m you reach a large roundabout, where you can turn left down to the beach at **Calella de Palafrugell** (1km there and back).

Otherwise, continue straight on along AVINGUDA DE JOAN PERICOT I GARCIA. After 500m you'll see the first sign for the **Jardí Botànic de Cap Roig★** (117.5km ✳🖼). This privately run cliff-top garden contains a wonderful display of Mediterranean, tropical and sub-tropical flora (open daily at 09.00; (972 614582). Retrace your route to the large roundabout (120.5km) and turn left along the dual carriageway to **Palafrugell** (124km *i♿⚓▲M*; tourist information (972 611820; weekly market Sunday morning), one of the main towns of the Costa Brava, where you can visit the Museu del Suro, dedicated to the local cork industry (closed Mondays and Sunday afternoons; (972 303998;

Short walks for motorists

Near Platja del Castell; right: Cistus crispus

crispus in May, then crosses a clearing to emerge on a track next to a bridge over the stream (**30min**). Turn right across the bridge (still on the GR), then right almost immediately onto another track, which will take you back to the entry road just where the tarmac ends in **40min**.

🚐14 Puig de les Cadiretes

3km/1.9mi; 50min. A quick 70m/ 230ft climb to one of the highest peaks (518m/1700ft) in the area — an ideal picnic spot, with wonderful views of the Alt and Baix Empordà, the Montseny and, on clear days, the heights of the eastern Pyrenees. Park as indicated at the 179.5km-point in the tour.

Walk southwards up a sandy track signposted GR-92 into the cork oak forest, where recently harvested trees — the corky bark is removed

🚐13 Platja del Castell

3km/1.9mi; 40min. A short circular stroll behind what is probably the best-preserved beach in this sector of the Costa Brava. Take swimwear and a picnic. Park at the end of the tarmac as described at the 133km-point in the tour.

From where the tarmac ends on the road to the *platja*, continue along the unsurfaced road to the beach — unspoilt and gloriously quiet out of season — to cross westwards over the mouth of the (usually dry) small stream that runs into the sea here (**15min**). Pick up an obvious path — the GR-92 — running north, parallel to the stream, looking out for little and cattle egrets roosting in the taller trees here. The route takes you through mixed pine and evergreen oak woodland, enlivened by an understorey of deep-crimson-flowered *Cistus*

every nine or ten years — show off their deep vermilion trunks. Following the GR WAYMARKS, ignore all tracks off left and right until you reach a fork (**15min**). Bear right, still on the GR, and come to a clearing where PUIG DE LES CADIRETES is clearly indicated to the right. Start to climb; then, in another clearing, follow the signposted path left all the way to the rocky summit of **Puig de les Cadiretes** (**25min**). Retrace your steps to return to your vehicle (**50min**).

e-mail: info@museudelsuro.org). From Palafrugell, continue to **Mont-ras** (127km), little more than a suburb of its larger neighbour, to pick up the main C31 again. This takes you inexorably closer to the charmless high-rise coastal sprawl located between Palamós and Sant Feliu de Guíxols.

At a roundabout (131km), turn left towards PLATJA DEL CASTELL, then follow the narrow road past Camping Benelux (△). The tarmac runs out just 700m short of the beach at **Platja del Castell** (133km ✳🏖13P), by far the most attractive and natural of the beaches on this stretch of the coast. Park here or further on just behind the beach to explore this idyllic spot, busy only at weekends or in high summer.

Return to the roundabout (135km) and turn left towards PALAMOS, once more along the C31. Just 1km further south, turn left off the C31 following signs to CENTRE URBÀ AND ZONA PORTUÀRIA, to reach the waterfront in **Palamós**★ (139km ⌂🏊🍴△M; tourist information ℓ 972 600550; weekly market Tuesday morning), an important commercial fishing port and thus an excellent place to sample seafood; try *arroç negre*, which is rice cooked in squid ink.

To leave Palamós, continue southwards, following signs to GIRONA and then SANT FELIU, to rejoin the C31 (142.5km). Bypass the ghastly high-rise sprawl of **Platja d'Áro** (*i*🏊🍴△✖🏪; tourist information ℓ 972 817179), of which the less said the better, and then take the *second* of the turn-offs to **Sant Feliu de Guíxols**★ (157km *i*🏊🍴△M; tourist information ℓ 972 820051; weekly market Sunday), a similar-sized town to Palamós but rather less 'touristy'. Enter the town along

the C65 and then continue along a long straight avenue. Turn right towards TOSSA (160.5km), then turn left (same signposting), to reach the Portada Ferrada — the name given (probably in reference to its arched entrance) to the Benedictine monastery and church, containing Romanesque, Gothic and Baroque elements. This houses the Museu d'Història de Sant Feliu de Guíxols (closed Mondays and Sunday afternoons; ℓ 972 821575). The old Baroque entrance arch into the monastery grounds, l'Arc de Sant Benet, stands alone just outside the buildings. Continue to the left of the monastery to reach the beach just 200m further on (161.5km), or go right towards TOSSA.

Once you've had your fill of Sant Feliu, return to the Portada Ferrada to pick up the road to TOSSA (GI682), spectacularly sinuous and passing through thick umbrella pine and cork and holm oak forests, always with the gleaming Mediterranean far down to your left. Around 11km further on, turn right towards LLAGOSTERA on the GIP6821 (173km). You pass the attractive whitewashed chapel of **Sant Grau d'Ardenya** after 5km, and 1.5km further on you reach a track off to your left (179.5km) marked by a GR-92 signpost. It leads up to the summit of the **Puig de les Cadiretes** (518m/1700ft ✳🏖🚗14P), a fine viewpoint over most of northeastern Catalonia.

Continue down into the unpretentious town of **Llagostera** (190km 🏊🍴✖🏪; weekly market Thursday), where the enormous Bar Casino in the main square is a step back in time and the perfect place for a drink towards the end of a hard day's touring. From Llagostera, follow the C65 north, back to **Girona** (210km — or 220km from the centre).

Tour 5: THE ALT EMPORDÀ PLAIN — INLAND FROM THE MADDING CROWDS

Figueres • Terrades • Mare de Déu de la Salut • Pantà de Boadella • Darnius • Agullana • Cantallops • Castell de Requesens • Cantallops • Estanys de Canadal • Capmany • Espolla • Coll de Banyuls • Espolla • Rabós • Sant Quirc de Colera • Garriguella • Vilajuïga • Castelló d'Empúries • Peralada • Vilabertran • Figueres

147km/91mi; 5-6 hours' driving (or 98.5km/61mi; 3-4 hours' driving via the alternative route)
En route: Walks 17, 18, 21, 22, 23; Short walk for motorists 🚗 15
The main tour follows a number of narrow, winding and poorly maintained surfaced roads and several sections along broad, well-maintained unsurfaced tracks. If you prefer not to drive on unsurfaced tracks, take the alternative route detailed in the footnote on page 42. Traffic is fairly light, even in the summer months; slow-moving farm vehicles and the busy junction on the NII between Agullana and Cantallops are the main hazards.
Picnic suggestions: Mare de Déu de la Salut (13.5km 🛋), river

Stripe-necked terrapin (Mauremys leprosa)

Muga (17.5km), **Pantà de Boadella** (21km, on the route of 🚗15), **Estanys de Canadal** (after 61km), **river Orlina** (after 73km and again at 95km), **Església de Santa Maria de Colera** (104km), **Mare de Déu del Camp** and the adjacent **Tortoise Recuperation Centre** (113.5km 🛋).

The *comarca* of Alt (upper) Empordà provides the setting for our day in the lowlands behind the rugged Costa Brava. We explore the thick evergreen oak forests which flourish in the foothills of Les Salines to the west of the main NII, the Serra de l'Albera and Cap de Creus, before touring a number of delightful medieval villages in the vicinity of Figueres.

We begin in well-appointed **Figueres★** (*i*☺🚻🏨🛆△M; lively Thursday morning market), internationally renowned for the Teatre-Museu Dalí shown on page 47. This houses an impressive collection of some of Salvador Dalí's most famous paintings and *objets d'art* (open daily 09.00-19.15 from July to September inclusive; the rest of the year 10.30-17.15 but closed Mondays); ℓ 972 677509; Fax: 972 501666; e-mail: tmgrups@dali-estate.org; www.salvador-dali.org).
To start the tour proper, leave

Figueres by heading towards France on the NIIa, starting the kilometre readings at the Campsa petrol station just 1km north of the town centre. Where the NIIa joins the NII Figueres bypass (1.5km), turn left on the GIP5107 towards LLERS (5km).
In **Llers** (✗), follow signs to TERRADES, now on the GI510, through an attractive mosaic of olive groves, pine woodland and cereal fields, with vast clumps of giant orchids on the verges in early spring. At the entrance to **Terrades** (12km ✗) turn right

towards ALBANYÀ, shortly turning right again towards BOADELLA D'EMPORDÀ along the GI504. This road climbs quickly to a small pass called the **Coll de la Salut** (13km). Just 200m further on, turn left to **Mare de Déu de la Salut** (13.5km ⓣ✕🏠P), where Walk 23 starts and finishes. This small sanctuary also boasts a restaurant (closed Fridays) and a pleasant picnic area.

Back on the GI504, wind north-wards down from the Coll de la Salut through Aleppo pine forest towards BOADELLA D'EMPORDÀ (✕). The village itself lies hidden to the right just where you cross over the **river Muga** (17.5km P), one of the cleanest watercourses in Catalonia, harbouring a thriving population of otters. (Follow a path upstream along the north bank of the river for 250m/yds to find a pleasant, shady picnic spot.) About 300m beyond the river, turn left and follow signposting to the PRESA. Park just next to the large dam at the **Pantà de Boadella** (21km ✳🗑wc🚗15P). The Short walk for motorists crosses the dam wall here.

From the reservoir, continue north through thick cork oak forests to the traffic lights on the edge of **Darnius** (24km △✕). The village centre is to the left, but turn right on the GI502. Then, just after crossing the **river Ricardell**, turn left on the GI504 (26.5km) towards AGULLANA. The nerve centre of **Agullana** (31km ⓣ♠✕M) is the Plaça Major, home to the 12th-century church of Santa Maria, with its two-tiered bell tower.

From Agullana pick up the GI500 signposted to FIGUERES and BARCELONA. Just after passing under the new high-speed rail line and the motorway, cross straight over the

Short walk for motorists

🚗15 Pantà de Boadella *2.5km/1.5mi; 40min; 80m/260ft of ascent/descent. An interesting circular route through a fine mature cork oak forest overlooking the banks of the Boadella reservoir. Park in the car park (with toilets) next to the dam, at the 21km-point in the tour.*

From the car park, walk across the dam and, on the far side, turn right immediately along a path-cum-track which hugs the bank of the **Pantà de Boadella** (good picnicking possibilities) and passes through a mature cork oak forest, accompanied by an abundance of strawberry-tree, *Phillyrea latifolia*, tree heath, sage-leaved cistus and French lavender. After **10min** the path begins to ascend quite steeply. When you meet a TRACK (**15min**), turn left uphill. Continue over a crest and down to a VIEWPOINT on your left with metal railings (**30min**). Look out here for the very common ocellated lizard and two interesting butterflies: Chapman's green hairstreak in spring and the beautiful two-tailed pasha in late summer/ autumn, whose caterpillars both feed on strawberry-tree leaves.

From here, pick up an old surfaced road which takes you east downhill to just beyond the dam. At this point botanists might like to carry straight on for 500m/yds, to look for creeping snapdragon and the rare fern *Pellaea calomelanos* on the rocks. Otherwise, turn left down another road, to cross back over the dam and return to the car park (**40min**).

Two-tailed pasha (Charaxes jasius)

41

NII (36km)* at a roundabout and continue towards CANTALLOPS on the GI601. Wind up steadily through a mature cork oak forest to reach **Cantallops** ('Wolf-Song'!; 42km ▲✗), where you should follow signs to REQUESENS. This unsurfaced road leads you in 7.5km to the remarkable **Castell de Requesens** (49.5km; open daily from 11.00 in summer but weekends only in winter; ✆ 972 193081). The castle was completely restored in the 20th century and today resembles an over-imaginative Hollywood film-set; it is also explored during the latter part of Walk 22.

Return to **Cantallops** (57km), then retrace your route along the GI601 towards the NII, turning left after 3.5km onto a good unsurfaced road signposted CONJUNT MEGALÍTIC DELS ESTANYS. This refers to the many prehistoric dolmens and menhirs (standing stones) which litter the area; most are signposted off the main **Conjunt Megalític dels Estanys**

*****Alternative route:** Follow the main tour to the 36km-point, then turn right along the NII towards FIGUERES. After 6km turn left on the GI502 to reach **Capmany** (45km) and rejoin the tour at the 63.5km-point. From here follow the main tour past **Sant Climent Sescebes** (52km) to **Espolla** (54.5km) and then, without entering the village, continue on the GI502 to pass **Rabós** (57.5km) on your left and then the hamlet of **Delfià** (60.5km ✳✿) on your right. Once at the crossroads with the C252 outside **Garriguella** (63.5km), turn left to enter the village and then follow signs to the CRT L'ALBERA, to reach the **Centre de Recuperació de la Tortuga de l'Albera**, where you definitively rejoin the main tour (64.5km).

route (🚶) you will follow from here on, but they are generally hard to find. Just 300m after the junction, park on the right next to a temporary lagoon: the first of the **Estanys de Canadal** (61km ✳☞P) which, in wet summers, are home to herons and marsh harriers, stripeless tree frogs and many dragonflies, including southern emerald damselflies, scarlet darters and Mediterranean hawkers, as well as aquatic plants such as amphibious bistort, bladderwort and lesser water-plantain; medicinal leeches were once exported to Britain from here!

Now continue southwards along this unsurfaced road and keep right at a fork after 200m. After another 400m you reach a farm next to the largest of the lagoons. From here continue to the right of the lagoon, bear left at another fork after 200m, then pass a second farm on your left after a further 1.5km. From this point continue straight on to **Capmany**★ (63.5km ✿▲✗). This pleasant village has three wine and champagne cellars to visit (for example, Celler Oliveda; ✆ 972 548006). In Capmany, pick up the GI602 left towards ROSES, passing through **Sant Climent Sescebes** (70.5km ▲✗). At **Espolla** (73km ℹ▲✗) follow signs to PAR. NATURAL ALBERA, to visit the information centre for the **Paratge Nacional de l'Albera** (open daily, but closed afternoons except Saturdays from June 1st to September 15th; ✆ 972 545079). From Espolla, pick up the road which heads roughly north towards the COLL DE BANYULS on the French border. This route traverses the foothills of the **Serra de l'Albera** (Monts d'Albères) and offers numerous picnic opportunities along the margins of the delightful **river Orlina**

(✳☞P). From the **Coll de Banyuls** (82km ☞) return the same way to **Espolla** (91km), then head southeast along the GI603 to the diminutive village of **Rabós** (94km ♨♠✕), clustered around the fortified Església de Sant Julià (13th-14th centuries).

Some 700m past Rabós, turn sharply back to the left towards SANT QUIRC DE COLERA (sometimes spelled 'Quirze'); then, after 400m, turn right along an unsurfaced road, again signposted to SANT QUIRC. This takes you over the **river Orlina** (P; a good picnic spot harbouring stripe-necked terrapins and golden orioles). Pass Rabós and a track down to the river on your left, then ascend to a small saddle before dropping down to a junction with another, even better, unsurfaced road (100km). Here turn left to reach the old Benedictine **Monestir de Sant Quirc** and the 10th-century **Església de Santa Maria de Colera** (104km ✳♨✕P), where Walk 21 starts and finishes. There is a rustic restaurant in amongst the group of buildings (closed Wednesdays; ☎ 972 193186). Retrace your route for 4km to the junction of unsurfaced roads (108km), this time keeping left towards VILAMANISCLE. Pass through **Vilamaniscle** (110km ♠✕) and pick up the GIV6032,

towards GARRIGUELLA. Some 200m before Garriguella (113km) turn left, to reach after 400m the **Centre de Recuperació de la Tortuga de l'Albera** (✳*i*M⊞P). The aim of this excellent recuperation centre is to conserve Hermann's tortoise, one of the Iberian Peninsula's rarest vertebrates (opens 10.00, but closed from November 1st to mid-March, when the tortoises are hibernating; a morning visit is recommended; ☎ 972 552245). Next to the centre is the small chapel of **Mare de Déu del Camp** (♨P). Both the grounds of the centre and the chapel environs make pleasant picnic spots. Follow the GIV6032 into **Garriguella** (✳♠△✕) and head south to the C252, where you turn left towards ROSES. After passing under the N260 the road becomes the GI610 (117km). You pass through **Vilajuïga** (118km; *where you could link up with Car tour 6*), **Pau** (120.5km ✕☎) and then **Palau-saverdera** (123km ✕). Here you turn right along the GI6103, signposted to the ESTANYS DE VILAÜT. Ignore a road off left after 1km; keep straight on to the Restaurant Aiguamolls at **Les Toroelles** (125.5km ✕), where Walk 18 starts and finishes. Continue along this minor road, crossing an area of the

The canonical church of Santa Maria in Vilabertran

Left: southern emerald damselfly (Lestes barbarus); *right: stripeless tree frog* (Hyla meridionalis); *bottom: ocellated lizard* (Lacerta lepida)

Aiguamolls Natural Park

known, for obvious reasons, as the 'Three Bridges' (and looking out for white storks, bitterns and rollers).

Walk 17 begins and ends in the pleasant market town of **Castelló d'Empúries** (132km *i*⛪ ⛰⛰ ⛪ △M; weekly market Tuesday morning; tourist information ☎ 972 156233). Park on the outskirts to visit the impressive Romanesque-Gothic church of Santa Maria de Castelló — known as the Cathedral of the Empordà — which emerges proudly from the centre of the labyrinth of narrow streets that comprises the old quarter.

Leave Castelló on the GIV6043 from the western side of the town, heading northwest towards PERA-LADA. Pass through **Vilanova de la Muga** (136km ⛪✕) and then cross over the Barcelona–France railway line and the N260 (139km) before coming to the well-preserved fortified village of **Peralada★** (141km ⁂*i*⛪⛰ ⛰⛰ ⛪ ✕M), home to a world-famous summer festival of classical music (details at www.festivalperalada. com or ☎ 93 2805868). Turn left at the first roundabout on the outskirts of Peralada towards VILABERTRAN (note the white storks' nests on either side of the road here — see photograph on page 113). Then park 500m further on at a second roundabout, on the southern edge of the village, to explore its

44

delightful maze of timeless alleys and small squares. Perhaps visit the very modern Museu de la Vila, with its interactive touch-screen guide to the whole of the Alt Empordà (open 10.00-14.00 and 16.00-21.00; closed Mondays in winter; ☎ 972 538840). Another site of interest here is the Castell de Peralada with its Museu del Vi and impressive library (guided visits six times a day in winter, eight times a day in summer). Continue from the car park towards FIGUERES on the C252 for a last stop at **Vilabertran** (145km ⛪✕). Just beyond the village, turn left to visit the splendid canonical church of Santa Maria and the attached remains of the fortified monastery, including a small cloister and the Palau Abacial, the latter one of the best examples of civil Gothic architecture in Catalonia (10.00-13.00 and 15.00-17.00; closed Mondays and Sundays mornings). From here **Figueres** is just 2km away (147km).

Tour 6: THE ESSENCE OF THE ALT EMPORDÀ — THE WILD COSTA BRAVA, COASTAL MARSHES AND SALVADOR DALÍ

Figueres • Vilajuïga • Sant Pere de Rodes • Port de la Selva • Cadaqués • Cap de Creus • Cadaqués • Roses • Montjoi • Aiguamolls de l'Empordà • Sant Pere Pescador • Empúries • Sant Tomàs de Fluvià • Sant Miquel de Fluvià • Figueres

158km/98mi, four hours' driving
En route: Walks 17, 19, 20; Short walks for motorists 🚗 16, 17, 18
The roads are good, if rather busy at weekends and around Roses and Cadaqués.

Picnic suggestions: Mas Ventós (17.5km 🌲), **Sant Pere de Rodes** (18.5km), **Riera de Romanyac** (32km), **Montjoi** (85km), **El Cortalet** (111km 🌲), river Fluvià (after 142km)

T his tour shows off the best of the coastal Alt Empordà — the wild, often windswept landscape of Cap de Creus and the bird-rich marshes of the Aiguamolls de l'Empordà — as well as the quietest of the rural inland villages. We visit Cadaqués, once home to Salvador Dalí, many of whose works were inspired by the landscapes we visit on this tour.

Leave **Figueres** (for information about the town see page 40) by heading northeast towards LLANÇÀ on the N260, beginning the kilometre readings as you pass under the NII Figueres bypass. Continue for 8km until you are indicated right to **Vilajuïga** (✕🍴). In this village pick up the GIP6041, signposted left towards MONESTIR DE ST PERE DE RODES 10. Wind up through an area affected by a serious forest fire in 1999, passing signs to dolmens (at 11km and 16km) and eventually reaching the picnic area of **Mas Ventós** (17.5km ✳🌲🚗16🌲P). About 1km further on, at a small pass, bear right towards the UNESCO World Heritage Site of **Sant Pere de Rodes★** (✳♂✕🌲MP). Park immediately or in the supervised car park 500m futher on. This magnificent 10th- to 12th-century Benedictine monastery (opens 10.00, closed Mondays; ℂ 972 387559) commands fabulous views northwards and also houses an information point for the **Parc Natural del Cap de Creus** (open daily 10.00-14.00 and 16.00-19.00, but closes earlier in winter; ℂ 972 193191).

Back at the small pass on the road from Vilajuïga, continue north down an unclassified (but broad and properly maintained) road to the coastal GI612 (27km), where you turn left and then immediately right for the last 700m into the quiet fishing village/resort of **Port de la Selva** (28km *i*🏠♠△✕🍴🚗17). Walk 20 starts here.

From Port de la Selva pick up the GI613 south towards CADAQUÉS; the road winds up into the bleak heartland of Cap de Creus. After about 4km, fork right on a track signposted RUBIÉS/TORRENTBO (32km). This leads you down to the **Riera de Romanyac** (✳P), one of the best-preserved gullies on the north side of Cap de Creus. Park on the right, 200m from the road, and wander southeast down the track and along the stream. Continuing along the road into the heart of Cap de Creus, turn left at the junction with the GI614 (35km) and drop down to the outskirts of **Cadaqués★** (45km *i*♂🏠♠△✕🍴M; tourist information ℂ 972 258315; weekly market Monday morning). Park in the large car park on your right at the entrance to the village, just beyond the left turn to Cap de Creus. This resort, where Walk 20

45

Short walk for motorists

⌂16 Castell de Sant Salvador de Verdera

5km/3.1mi; 1h45min; 210m/690ft of ascent and descent. A linear walk via the famous monastery of Sant Pere de Rodes to the ruined castle of Sant Salvador, perched on all but the highest point of the Cap de Creus peninsula (670m/2200ft). Park at the Mas Ventós picnic site (17.5km).

From the **Mas Ventós** car park, head down the steps and take the track left which circumnavigates a pinewood with picnic tables (⊼). After 200m/yds, at a T-junction, turn left. After another 100m turn right towards SANTA HELENA. Follow this track steadily eastwards uphill until a sign indicating Santa Helena (**20min**) points you left, up and over a crest. You drop down quickly to the interesting pre-Romanesque chapel of **Santa Helena** (**25min**). From here bear right to pick up the road to the **Monestir de Sant Pere de Rodes** (**35min**).

Walk towards the monastery, but instead of entering, follow the path up to the right alongside a WOODEN HAND-RAIL. This path initially enters an extremely eroded, gully-like section, before zigzagging steeply up a rocky ridge to the ruins of the **Castell de Sant Salvador** (**1h**). From here there are excellent views south to

the Empordà plain and north into French Catalonia. Retrace your steps to the MONASTERY (**1h25min**) and then to **Mas Ventós** (**1h45min**).

Santa Helena (top), Castell de Sant Salvador (middle), and (bottom) view from Santa Helena to Sant Pere de Rodes (see also photograph page 10, taken from near the Castell de Sant Salvador).

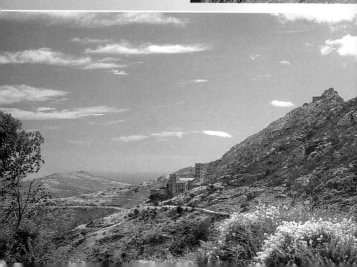

ends, still retains an air of tranquillity, despite its international fame as an artistic centre — aside from Dalí, it also inspired artists and musicians as disparate as Picasso, André Breton, Andrés Segovia and John Cage. The main highlights are the municipal Museu de Cadaqués, an art gallery with exhibitions in the summer focusing on Dalí (open daily from 10.30-13.30 and 15.00-20.00; ☎ 972 258877) and the Centre d'Art Perrot-Moore (open 11.00-13.30 and 16.30-20.30; closed Sundays; ☎ 972 258231), which houses a collection of works by Dalí and Picasso amassed by Dalí's former secretary and dealer.

Many of the local fishermen still speak a Mallorcan dialect of Catalan, a hangover from the days when it was easier to reach Mallorca by sea than to cross the thickly wooded Cap de Creus to Figueres — hence the name Port de la Selva ('Port of the Jungle').

Opposite the car park, pick up the unclassified road towards CAP DE

Teatre-Museu Dalí in Figueres

CREUS, keeping straight on at a crossroads after 1km (*or turn left here to go straight to Cap de Creus*). Following signs to CASA S DALÍ, turn sharp left, right and left again in quick succession, before reaching the beach at **Portlligat★** (46km ⛺🏔️⛵✕M), internationally famous for the Casa-Museu Salvador Dalí (entry only with a reservation, 10.30-18.00; ☎ 972 251015; Fax: 972 251083). Follow the road-cum-track behind the beach and pick up a corrugated concrete road signposted CENTRE VILA and then CADAQUÉS, to meet the road from Cadaqués to Cap de Creus 1km further on (47km). Turn right here for a spectacular drive across the windswept peninsula to the lighthouse (*far*) perched on the easternmost tip of **Cap de Creus** (53km ☀️☞✕), and, indeed, of the whole Iberian Peninsula. (The final stretch of Walk 20 follows the whole of this road, but in reverse.)

Retrace your route to **Cadaqués** and pick up the GI614 back towards PORT DE LA SELVA, but this time fork left (65km) towards ROSES. Some 9km further on, after a long descent with wonderful views south over the Alt Empordà plain, fork left again towards ROSES. In just over 2km you arrive at unattractive **Roses** (76km *i*⛺🏔️△). Turn left at the first roundabout, then continue straight across at the next two roundabouts, until you see a sign on the left indicating CALA MONTJOY 7 (the Castilian Spanish spelling of 'Montjoi'). Follow this road as it ascends an attractive valley past the largest dolmen in the area, **La Creu d'en Cobertella** (79km ⛩️), before reaching the end of the tarmac at **Montjoi** (85km *P*). Walk 19 starts and finishes here — at the gateway to the rugged coastline of cliffs and coves that delineates the southern

Short walks for motorists

🚗17 Cala Fornells

5km/3.1mi; 1h20min; repeated short climbs and descents totalling approximately 100m/230ft on rugged terrain.
This coastal footpath is the only practical way of reaching this remote sector of the northern coastline of Cap de Creus by land. After many ups and downs you reach the secluded Cala Fornells, a good bathing spot. Take swimwear. *Park near the harbour in Port de la Selva (28km in the tour). See map on page 124.*

From **Port de la Selva** follow the notes for Walk 20 on page 122 and round the headland of **Punta de la Creu** to the crossroads, where you should turn *left* downhill to the beach of **Cala Tamariua** (**10min**). On the far side of the cove pick up a narrow path, braided in places, which closely follows the extremely rugged coastline north and east as best it can. Rocky inlet succeeds rocky inlet and at times you will have to rely on your intuition to tell which is the best route onwards. After 20 minutes of glorious coastline, **Cap Mitjà** (**30min**) provides a fine viewpoint northwards, and from here the path continues much as before to the natural amphitheatre of **Cala Fornells** (**40min**); *take care on the final descent to the cove itself.* Here the coastal path finishes as the terrain becomes too sheer to negotiate although, amazing as it might seem, the area was once cultivated, with the abandoned terraces just discernible behind the beach.
Retrace your steps to **Port de la Selva** (**1h20min**).

🚗18 The banks of the river Fluvià

4km/2.5mi; 1h. This walk along the right bank of river Fluvià takes you down to the mouth of the river and a quiet section of beach where black-winged stilts and Kentish plovers breed in the dune-slacks. Park overlooking the river: at the 114.5km-point in the tour, head left towards 'Càmping La Gaviota'. After 100m, where the road bears right, keep straight on along a track past an 'Aiguamolls de l'Empordà' sign. Park after 400m in any convenient space.

Once at the river, walk east along the track, passing on your left the **Illa d'en Caramany**, an island created by the cutting of a new channel in 1979 with the aim of reducing erosion to the right bank of the Fluvià. Today it is a *reserva integral* and an excellent locality in which to observe breeding herons, plus ospreys and cormorants in winter. As the track turns right after 1km/0.6mi, continue straight on along paths, keeping close to the river bank. You will reach the BEACH after **30min**. Follow the track south behind the beach, to where a track enters from the right under a red and white MAXIMUM HEIGHT ARCH. Follow this track as it heads inland past an old farm, to pick up your original track along the **banks of the Fluvià**, where you turn left to return to your starting point (**1h**).

Photographs: southern white admiral (Limenitis reducta), top, and scarce swallowtail (Iphiclides podalirius), below

part of Cap de Creus. Picnic spots abound.

Retrace your route to Roses (96km), then follow signs to FIGUERES. Beyond Roses, you pass a series of ugly holiday complexes on the left. At a large roundabout on the outskirts of **Castelló d'Empúries** (107km *i⛵💧🏨▲△M*) turn left along the GIV6216 towards SANT PERE PESCADOR. Head south for 3km, then turn left where signposted to visit the most important part of the **Aiguamolls de l'Empordà** nature reserve, parking at the information centre of **El Cortalet** (111km ✳WC🅿*P*; open daily from 09.30-14.00 and 16.30-19.00; ✆ 972 454222; www.castellodempuries.net/ang/aigua/home.htm). All versions of Walk 17 pass through this point.

Back on the GIV6216, turn left to **Sant Pere Pescador** (114km 🏨▲△✕🅿) and continue straight through the village and over the **river Fluvià**, then turn left towards PLATGES at a roundabout just past the bridge. Within 500m, turn right at the next roundabout towards SANT MARTÍ D'EMPÚRIES (or left towards CÀMPING LA GAVIOTA for 🚗18). Follow this unclassified road through numerous orchards and past Camping Las Dunas, identified by its horrendous blue-painted discotheque. Just after crossing an area of marshland and the **Riu Vell**, you reach a large roundabout on the outskirts of the village of **Sant Martí d'Empúries**★ (117.5km 💧✕🅿WC), once the capital of the Empordà region, but today most famous for the Graeco-Roman ruins of **Empúries** (🏛M), one of the main entry ports to the Iberian Peninsula in ancient times. To visit both the ruins and the attached Museu d'Arqueologia (open daily from 10.00; ✆ 972 770208), park in the car park just beyond the

roundabout and walk south along the shady promenade behind the beach for 600m/yds to one entrance (open from June to September), or carry on for a further 200m to a hotel, where you turn inland to reach the main entrance as indicated.

From the roundabout at Sant Martí (117.5km) follow signs to L'ESCALA (now on the GIP6307), then turn right after 2km at another large roundabout (119km) onto the GI623 towards FIGUERES. As you approach **Viladamat** (126km), keep following signs towards FIGUERES, to pick up the main C31 northwards, which will take you to **Torroella de Fluvià** (132km). Here turn left towards SANT MIQUEL DE FLUVIÀ along the GIV6216 and detour right after 2km to **Sant Tomàs de Fluvià** (135km 💧). The squat Romanesque church on the left at the entrance to the village (once an Augustinian priory) possesses lovely 12th-century murals (visit only on Fridays 16.00-20.00 or Sundays from 12.00 onwards). Back on the GIV6216, once in **Sant Miquel de Fluvià** (137km 💧), visit the magnificent church with its sturdy bell-tower and important interior sculptures (only open on Sunday mornings). The road meanders on from Sant Miquel through pleasant wooded countryside and crosses the **river Fluvià** to reach **Sant Morí** (139km). Turn right here towards BÀSCARA and, in **Vilaür** (142km), turn right again towards GARRIGÀS. This delightful road crosses the Fluvià again (*P*) just south of **Arenys d'Empordà**, before passing through the quaint old village of **Garrigàs** (148km) and reaching the main NII (150km) just 8km south of **Figueres** (158km).

❋ Walking

Catalonia boasts an exceptional variety of landscapes, flora and fauna, which we have tried to reflect in our choice of walks for this book. We feel that the purpose of a walk is not to simply reach your destination, but rather to enjoy the scenery and wildlife along the way; thus, without having to travel too far, the 23 walks and their variants will take you along rocky and sandy shores, through the dense carpets of Mediterranean garrigue, beneath the shade cast by magnificent forests of evergreen oaks and beech and up to flower-rich subalpine pastures at the foot of peaks commanding stunning views.

Most of the walks in this book are within the capability of any reasonably fit person, although very occasionally there is a risk of vertigo. Of course, you must take the season and weather conditions into account before you set out: for example, high summer temperatures may make the lowland walks extremely uncomfortable at this time of year, while some of the routes through the higher mountains may be snowbound in winter. In addition, low-lying cloud may make route-finding difficult, as well as obscuring all the best views. **Remember too that storm damage can create hazardous conditions for walking** *at any time*.

If you are not an experienced walker you may like to cut your teeth on some of the Short walks for motorists described in the car tours before progressing to the main walks.

M aps

The maps in this book have been adapted from the latest 1:50,000 *mapes comarcals* which the Catalan government has published for each administrative region (*comarca*). If you wish to supplement our maps, you might like to consider those published by Edicions Alpina (www. editorialalpina.com) — the staple maps of Catalan walkers for many years; recent editions are generally very reliable.

Many of these maps will be available from your local stockist but, if you are in Catalonia, the best places to buy all types of maps are the shops belonging to the Institut Cartogràfic de Catalunya. In **Barcelona** their shop is located at C/ Balmes 209-211; in **Girona** at C/ Emili Grahit 10ª. More information is available on the website of the Institut Cartogràfic (www.icc.es). Also worth a visit are the Catalan government's official bookshops:

Barcelona: Rambla dels Estudis, 118; 08002 Barcelona
  Tel: 93 3026462; Fax: 93 3186221;
  e-mail: llibrbcn@correu.cattel.com
Girona: Gran Via de Jaume I, 38; 17001 Girona
  Tel: 972 22 72 67; Fax: 972 227315;
  e-mail: llibrgi@ibernet.com
Another good bookshop is Altaïr, located at Gran Via de les
Corts Catalans, 616; 08007 Barcelona, which specialises in
maps and travel and wildlife books and has an on-line
ordering service at www.altair.es.

Waymarking

The Catalans have a long tradition of waymarking
trails and footpaths, traditionally with small cairns or other
essentially natural elements. During the 1970s and 1980s,
however, many paths in areas such as Sant Llorenç del Munt
(Walk 4) were haphazardly marked with paint of every
conceivable colour, each local walking group deciding more
or less at random where and how to do so. Nevertheless, in
recent years waymarking has been standardised: discreet red
and white stripes represent a GR route *(sender de gran
recorregut)*, yellow and white stripes a PR *(sender de petit
recorregut)* and green and white stripes an SL *(sender local)*;
standardised signposts, such as those used in the Montseny
and Garrotxa natural parks, are also on the increase.

As their Catalan name implies, GRs are *long-distance routes*
of over 50km; PRs *(short-distance routes)* may be anything
between 10 and 50 km; SLs *(local routes)* usually fall short of
10km. While you can usually trust the accuracy of their
painted waymarks, there is no guarantee that these paths will
be *easy*; some, especially the longer ones, traverse quite
difficult terrain, and *care should be taken if you decide to follow a
waymarked route not described in this book*. As of autumn 2006,
a number of paths in the Garrotxa and Alt Empordà regions
(for example, part or all of Walks 8, 9, 10, 11, 12, 20, 21, 22,
and 23) will be waymarked with a yellow flash, the logo of a
new network of historical footpaths created by the local
tourist boards. It is also important to be familiar with the
international code for waymarking.

In many cases the walks in this book follow waymarked
trails, as these traverse some of the most scenic areas in Catalonia. The route descriptions, however, have been written as
if the waymarks *didn't* exist, in case the tree or stone with the
crucial paint has fallen or been removed in the interim! Nevertheless, where such waymarks are present, they are referred
to in the text.

Where to stay

Rural tourism has really taken off in Catalonia. There are plenty of options for finding lodgings and a hot meal in even the most remote areas. In the 1980s, the Catalan government began to promote a network of *cases de pagès* — small farms which would provide food and accommodation as a means of supplementing their often rather meagre and irregular income. The (in)famous cheap and cheerful *fonda, hostal* or *pensió* still exists, while campsites can often be found in quite remote localities, but are generally only open at weekends and/or in the summer.

The Catalan government has published a series of guides to all hotels, *cases de pagès* and campsites, which can be purchased at the bookshops mentioned above and elsewhere. The following websites may help you to find accommodation before you travel: www.agronet.org/agroturisme and www.casesdepages.com. Among the larger towns, Barcelona is obviously the best centre for Walks 1-7, Olot is the ideal choice when visiting the Garrotxa (Walks 8-12), and Girona and Figueres are well placed for Walks 13-23, which explore the Costa Brava and its immediate hinterland.

Weather hints

The Mediterranean climate of Catalonia is characterised above all by its stability. Atlantic fronts usually blow themselves out well before they reach the coast and, especially in summer and winter, anticyclones — and their accompanying clear skies — sit over the country for days on end. On the other hand, the northern Costa Brava is notorious for a strong northerly wind — *la tramuntana* — which blows cold and hard off the plains of Roussillon in France for days on end, especially in autumn and winter. For comfort's sake, Walks 18-23 are not recommended if there is a *tramuntana*.

In general, **September to June** are the best months for walking, as temperatures in **July** and **August** will be unbearable for most people. Even so, **spring** and **autumn** temperatures can creep up towards 30°C, and on mild **winter** days may reach a pleasant 20°C on the coast. Summer temperatures on the coast are usually cooler than just inland, thanks to the *marinada*, an onshore breeze that picks up in the afternoons. On the highest inland walks, temperatures will rarely climb above 25°C, even in high summer, but don't forget that insolation increases considerably with altitude; be prepared with sunhat, high-factor suncream and sunglasses. By contrast, you *could* encounter sub-zero temperatures and snow between **November and May** in the Montseny and on

Puigsacalm, while Montserrat and Sant Llorenç will also get the occasional dusting of snow in **winter**.

January is the second-*driest* month of the year in much of Catalonia, as the region's winter weather is often characterised by powerful anticyclones providing stable, dry conditions. There may be overnight frost, but it will be warm enough to walk in short sleeves by midday. Rain, when it comes, is largely a **spring or autumn** phenomenon, very often in the form of violent thunderstorms. Getting caught in a storm at high altitude is a not-to-be-recommended experience, as up to 100 litres/m^2 can fall in an hour. If you get caught in such a storm, try to find a hut or cave for shelter and, above all, *avoid dry river beds and gullies*.

For those with internet access, the Digital Climatic Atlas of Catalonia (http://magno.uab.es/atles-climatic) provides monthly average rainfall, insolation and temperature figures for the whole of Catalonia, in Catalan, Spanish and English.

Clothing and equipment

Walking in Catalonia is really no different from walking in any other country: you *must* take a minimum of equipment (indicated in the introduction to each walk) and *should* carry as much of the supplementary equipment listed below as possible, to be on the safe side. All reasonable-sized towns have sports or outdoor shops where you can buy equipment.

On rough terrain there is *absolutely no substitute* for walking boots, as you will need to rely on the grip and ankle support, as well as their waterproof qualities. Some of the walks in this book involve muddy tracks, paths with loose stones, and descents along slippery cobbles, and the only footwear able to cope with such a variety of conditions is waterproof boots with proper soles. Where we suggest that 'stout shoes' are sufficient, these must be of the lace-up variety with thick rubber or 'Vibram-type' soles to provide a good grip.

You may find the following checklist useful:

— adequate footwear: boots (which *must* be broken in and comfortable) or stout shoes, unless otherwise stated in the walk introduction
— waterproof raingear (all year round, as sudden thunderstorms are not uncommon)
— long-sleeved shirt (for sun protection, especially for those unused to long hours in the sun, by the sea or on high-altitude walks)
— fleece or jersey or any other type of removable cold-weather clothing
— gloves and warm hat (at altitude or in the winter)
— spare bootlaces; extra pair of socks
— sunhat, sunglasses and protective suncream
— first aid kit, including plasters, bandages, an antiseptic of some kind and aspirin (some things, such as antiseptic cream or antiseptic wipes may not be available in Catalonia)
— compass and additional maps

— picnic kit (penknife with tin and bottle openers, plastic utensils)
— whistle, matches, small torch, mobile phone
— water bottle and water-purifying tablets
— insect repellent
— Dog Dazer (see under 'Dogs') or a stout stick
— small rucksack with pockets.

Please note that we've not done *every* walk in this book under *all* weather conditions: use your judgement to modify the above list accordingly. In hot weather *always* wear a sunhat and apply suncream sensibly. Don't forget your sunglasses if you are venturing out while there is still snow on the ground.

Dogs — and other nuisances

Most Catalan farmhouses have **watchdogs**; their bark is intended to warn their owners of the approach of strangers, rather than scare people off. We have made every effort to ensure that no walk in this book passes through farms with loose dogs of any size that might bite. If a barking farm dog is preventing you from continuing along the path, just wait and usually the owner will come out to see what all the fuss is about. If you have any doubts, carry a stout stick or a Dog Dazer (an ultrasonic device than frightens dogs away without harming them; these are sold by Sunflower Books).

Sheepdogs, on the other hand, are occasionally a bit over-zealous when guarding their flocks and may be rather intimidating, even though the typical Catalan sheepdog is about half the size of a mastiff or Alsatian. If you make your presence known to the shepherd (look under the nearest shady tree!), a quick word from him or her will control the dogs.

Catalonia is not a country of wild fighting bulls, but rather one of many herds of cows, sometimes accompanied by the odd **bull**, although these latter are generally quite peaceable in the company of their 'harem'. Despite their horns and their short-sightedness, **cows** are harmless *unless* they are with their calves; *never* get between a cow and her calf, and if in doubt, skirt the whole herd. These free-grazing cattle are most commonplace in upland areas (above all on Walks 7, 9, 21 and 22), but may also be found deep in the woods (!), where they often stand in the middle of the track; be patient, or just find a way around them.

The only large wild beasts, aside from deer, to roam the woods of Catalonia today are the highly abundant **wild boar**, but they are so wary of humans that, unless you are incredibly lucky, you will not see or even hear one. Their human predators are another matter, however, as **hunting** is a widespread winter activity, practised across almost all the area covered by this book, including the natural parks (although not in the

Aiguamolls where Walks 17 and 18 are based). The season lasts from October to mid-February, at weekends and on Thursdays and public holidays. If you hear shots close at hand or if you think you are being mistaken for a potential target, a quick shout (even in English!) will soon make the issue clear.

Be more wary of **snakes**. Of the venomous species found in Catalonia, the asp is widespread, so avoid walking through thick undergrowth or open rocky areas wearing sandals or with bare legs. Less dangerous but somewhat larger is the Montpellier snake, which reaches lengths of over 2m/6.5ft and will occasionally put its head up and hiss before slithering away. Its bite is very painful, but no more. Small **scorpions** live under stones in many dry areas and can give you a nasty sting; likewise, a black- and yellow-striped **centipede**, also to be found under stones, has a vicious bite. You will, of course, come across **mosquitoes**, **clegs** and other biting insects, although liberal amounts of insect repellent will generally do the trick.

Your fellow human beings can at times be rather more hazardous than the native wildlife. Groups of **4WDs**, 'quads' (four-wheeled **motorbikes**) and **trail bikes** migrate in packs to the countryside from Barcelona at weekends. Galling as it may be, if you hear a motorised vehicle coming your way make sure that you stand well clear of the path to let it pass, as you are bound to come off worse if any contact is made.

General advice to walkers

The following points cannot be stressed too often.

- **At any time a walk may become unsafe due to storm damage or bulldozing**. If the route differs from the description in the book, or your way ahead is not clear, do not attempt to continue.
- **Walks above 1000m/3300ft may be hazardous in winter**, when the route may be obscured by snow; all routes can be dangerous in poor visibility, when there is a very real chance of losing your way.
- **Warm clothing** is always needed in the high mountains, even in summer.
- **Never walk alone**: four is the best number for a walking group. If someone is injured, two can go for help and there is no need for anyone to be left alone.
- **Do not overestimate your capability**: the Catalan terrain is very abrupt. Aside from Walks 17 and 18, *all walks* involve some ascent and/or descent, often on narrow paths and trails. If in doubt, begin with one of the Short walks for motorists, or do just part of a walk. Keep a careful eye on the time, to complete the walk before sunset and/or pick up your transport connection, and remember: your speed will be determined by the slowest member of the group.
- **Bus/train connections** at the end of a linear walk may be vital. Always check departure times *before* setting out.
- **Adequate footwear** is imperative.

- **Mists** can suddenly appear at higher elevations, when a **compass** might make the difference between life and death.
- Similarly, a **first-aid kit, whistle, torch, knife,** mobile phone weigh little and take up next to no space in your rucksack, but might save your life. The international emergency number in Europe is 112.
- **Sufficient water** must be carried at all times, especially in summer. We recommend that you take at least 1 litre per person for the average 3-4 hour walk on a warm day; more for those who sweat more, for longer walks or for hotter days. The many *fonts* referred to in the walks generally take the form of a natural spring channelled into a pipe, often set in elaborate stone or brick structures; this water is safe to drink, unless it actually says '*no potable*'.
- **Extra rations** must be taken on longer walks.
- Always follow the **Countryside code** on page 12; read carefully the 'Important note' on page 2 and the guidelines on grade and equipment for each walk you are planning.

Language hints

The first language of the vast majority of people who you will meet on your walks is Catalan, a Romance language which is as close to French as it is to Castilian Spanish. Although everybody also speaks Spanish as well, you will hear little spoken in rural Catalonia, and this brief list of useful Catalan phrases will stand you in good stead.

English	Catalan	Approximate pronunciation
Hello	*Hola*	*Oh-lah*
Good morning	*Bon dia*	*Bon **dee**-er*
Good afternoon	*Bona tarda*	***Bon**-er **tard**-er*
I am lost.	*Estic perdut.*	*Ehs-**tick** pur-**doot**.*
Please ...	*Si us plau ...*	*Si oos **plau***
Where is ...	*On és ...*	*On ehs ...*
the road to ...?	*la carretera a ...?*	*la ka-ret-er-er ah ...?*
the path to ...?	*el camí a ...?*	*ul ker-**mi** ah ...?*
the bus stop?	*la parada del bus?*	*la per-**rah**-der dul bus?*
Is there a bar here?	*Hi ha cap bar aquí?*	*Ee ah cap bar er-**key**?*
Is there a taxi here?	*Hi ha cap taxista aquí?*	*Ee ah cap tax-**ist**-er er-**key**?*
May I use the phone?	*Puc trucar?*	*Pook true-**car**?*
Many thanks.	*Moltes gràcies.*	***Moul**-ters grah-si-ahs.*
Is this the way?	*És per aquí?*	*Ehs pair eh-**key**?*
Is it over there?	*És cap allà?*	*Ehs cap eh-**yar**?*
Is it straight ahead?	*És tot recte?*	*Ehs tot **rec**-ter?*
Is it to the left?	*És cap a l'esquerra?*	*Ehs cap ah lers-**ker**-rer?*
Is it to the right?	*És cap a la dreta?*	*Ehs cap ah la **dre**-ter?*
Is it behind?	*És per darrera?*	*Ehs purr de-**rare**-rer?*
Is it above?	*És per amunt?*	*Ehs purr er-**munt**?*
Is it below?	*És per abaix?*	*Ehs purr er-**bash**?*
Take us to ... (place)	*Porti'ns a ...*	***Port**-ins ah ...*
Come and pick us up	*Vingui a buscar-nos*	***Bing**-ee ah buss-**car**-noose*
at 7 o'clock (time*).	*a les set.*	*ah lers set.*
at the bar (place**).	*al bar.*	*ul bar.*

*Just point out on your watch the time you wish to be collected; **name the village/landmark — such as the church (*ehs-**gle**-see-ah*), information point (***sen**-trer din-for-mass-ee-oh*) or one of the terms in the Glossary opposite.

Glossary

Catalan maps are littered with topographical references, some of which we have used in this book. Below is a useful vocabulary, with approximate pronunciation (plurals with 's', unless otherwise indicated.

Catalan	Approximate pronunciation	English
aguait	ah-**gwhite**	hide
aiguamolls	ah-gwer-mols	fresh-water marshes
bassa/basses	**bah**-sir	pool
cala/cales	**ka**-ler	cove
camí/camins	ker-**mee**	track, road, path
cap	**cap**	headland
carrer	ker-**ray**	street
castell	kah-**stay**	castle
cingla/cingles	**sing**-ler	cliff
codina/codines	koo-**dee**-ner	bare, flat area or rock
coll	**kohl**	pass or saddle
collada/collades	kohl-**ya**-der	pass or saddle
collet	koohl-**yet**	small pass
ermita/ermites	er-**mee**-ter	chapel
estany	ers-**tang**	lake
fageda/fagedes	fer-**djai**-der	beech forest
font	**fon**	spring
gola/goles	**goh**-ler	mouth of river
illa/illes	**eel**-ya	island
llac	**yak**	lake
masia/masies	meh-**see**-ah	farmhouse
massís/massissos	meh-**sees**	massif
mirador	mee-ra-**door**	look-out point
molí/molins	moo-**lee**	mill
monestir	moo-nes-**teer**	monastery
pantà/pantans	pehn-**tar**	reservoir
pic	**peeck**	peak
pista/pistes	**pees**-the	track
platja/platjes	**pla**-dja	beach
pont	**pon**	bridge
puig	**pooch**	mountain
rasos	**rah**-zoos	upland pasture
riera/rieres	ree-**ay**-rah	stream
riu	**ree**-oo	river
santuari	san-too-**ah**-ree	sanctuary
salt	**sal**	waterfall
sender	sehn-**day**	path
serra/serres	**seh**-rah	ridge
serralada/serralades	seh-reh-**lah**-deh	large ridge
torrent	too-**ren**	gully
turó/turons	too-**roh**	peak
val	**bal**	valley

Organisation of the walks

The 23 walks in this book have been divided into three groups: Walks 1-7 are within easy reach of **Barcelona**, Walks 8-12 are centred on the town of Olot in the **Garrotxa** region, inland from the Costa Brava, and Walks 13-23 are very much linked to the **Costa Brava and its immediate hinterland**, best reached from Figueres and/or Girona.

When planning a walk, you might start by looking at the large fold-out map inside the back cover, which shows you at a glance the general terrain, the road network and the location of the walks that are nearest to you. Then turn to the route notes and the accompanying large-scale maps.

Each walk is described in the direction which we feel is the most attractive and poses the fewest transport problems (any ascents usually come early on in the route). Feel free to try them in reverse. Standard terminology has been used: **roads** are metalled, **unsurfaced roads** are passable in ordinary cars, **tracks** are only suitable for 4WDs, **paths** are too narrow for vehicles, and **trails** are old paths or tracks which still retain some of their original paving.

To give you an idea of the settings of the various walks, there is at least one photograph for each.

Each itinerary begins with planning information: distance, grade, necessary equipment and details of access. Pay particular attention where we refer to the ascent: although the average walker may be able to tackle 600m/2000ft without too much difficulty, extreme temperatures may make the route harder than you imagine; anything more requires a higher level of fitness. **Times** are given for various landmarks en route, but bear in mind that everyone walks at a different pace and that your speed will also vary according to the load you are carrying, the time of day, weather conditions, etc. As a rule of thumb, calculate 13 minutes for every kilometre on the flat, plus an additional 13 minutes for every 100m of ascent. Bear in mind as well that some of the more difficult *descents* may also slow you up. No time for stops is included, so make sure that you allow plenty of extra time for lunch, swimming, birdwatching or botanising and photography.

The following **symbols** are used on the walking maps:

motorway	spring, waterfall, etc	castle, fort.in ruins
main road	church.chapel	building
secondary road	shrine or cross	watchtower.cave
minor or untarred road	cemetery	hide
track.path or trail	picnic tables	quarry, mine
main walk.alternative	best views	stadium.campsite
natural park boundary	bus stop	ice pit
short walk for motorists	car parking	map continuation
height in metres	railway station	picnic suggestion

Walk 1: MARE DE DÉU DE BRUGUERS • CASTELL D'ERAMPRUNYÀ • PUIG DE LES AGULLES • LA MORELLA • LA PLETA • GARRAF

Distance: 14km/8.7mi; 3h50min (Alternative descent to Platja de Castelldefels 4h35min)

Grade: two ascents, the first of 312m/1025ft (including a short, sharp initial climb) and then another of 116m/380ft, plus a long descent of 596m/1955ft, all combined with a lack of shade and stony paths, make this a fairly strenuous walk. The route follows two versions of the GR-92 throughout and is feasible all year round except summer.

Equipment: boots or stout shoes, *sunhat*, long-sleeved garment, long trousers (to combat the prickly scrub!), raingear, picnic, water

Access: 🚌 to Gavà (20km via the C32 motorway from Barcelona), or 🚆 (RENFE; four trains per hour), then 🚐 (Timetable 1); ask to be put off at Mare de Déu de Bruguers. Return by 🚆 (RENFE) from Garraf station to Gavà or Barcelona at 54 minutes past the hour (or from Platja de Castelldefells railway station at 28 and 58 minutes past the hour for the Alternative descent).

Short walk: Mare de Déu de Bruguers — Castell d'Eramprunyà — Puig de les Agulles — Mare de Déu de Bruguers. 8km/5mi; 2h40min. Easy, but still with 312m/1025ft of ascent; access, equipment and season as above. Follow the main walk as far as the 1h25min-point and return the same way.

Despite its proximity to Barcelona, this excursion across the low but highly scenic hills of the Garraf provides something for walkers and wildlifers alike. The early part of the walk traverses reddish siliceous rock, populated by narrow-leaved cistus, ling and, more rarely, the attractive yellow-flowered *Halimium halimifolium*. The predominant bedrock of the Garraf, however, is pale, highly karstified limestone, where extravagantly tall clumps of *Ampelodesmos mauritanica* — a grass which has naturally colonised parts of southern Europe from Africa — emerge from a dense carpet of holly oak, rosemary, shrubby globularia and the winter-flowering heather *Erica multiflora*.

The red cliffs of the Garraf above Bruguers

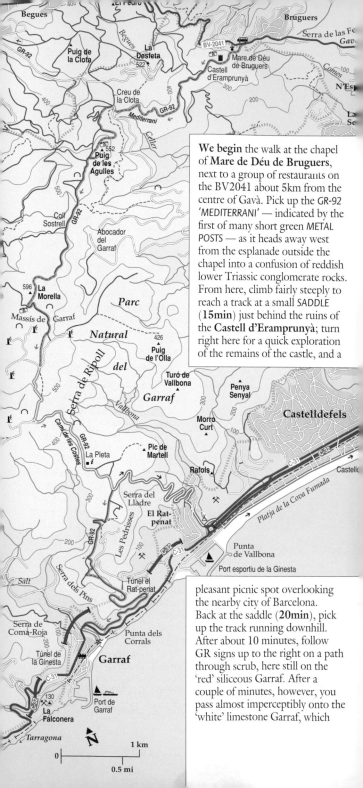

We begin the walk at the chapel of **Mare de Déu de Bruguers**, next to a group of restaurants on the BV2041 about 5km from the centre of Gavà. Pick up the GR-92 'MEDITERRANI' — indicated by the first of many short green METAL POSTS — as it heads away west from the esplanade outside the chapel into a confusion of reddish lower Triassic conglomerate rocks. From here, climb fairly steeply to reach a track at a small SADDLE (**15min**) just behind the ruins of the **Castell d'Eramprunyà**; turn right here for a quick exploration of the remains of the castle, and a

pleasant picnic spot overlooking the nearby city of Barcelona. Back at the saddle (**20min**), pick up the track running downhill. After about 10 minutes, follow GR signs up to the right on a path through scrub, here still on the 'red' siliceous Garraf. After a couple of minutes, however, you pass almost imperceptibly onto the 'white' limestone Garraf, which will be underfoot for much of the remainder of the walk. Some 20 minutes later, you reach **Creu de la Clota** (**1h**), an open saddle with a junction of tracks. This is a surprisingly good spot for butterflies, considering the extremely arid nature of the Garraf. In June, for example, literally thousands of false ilex hairstreaks nectar on the yellow blossoms of the everlasting flower *Helichrysum stoechas*, together with scarce swallowtails, Cleopatras, Provence chalk-hill and Escher's blues and marbled skippers, to name but a few. Look out too for the handsome *Zygaena lavandulae* here — a black burnet moth with a white collar.

Cross the saddle and take the white gravel track left into the Aleppo pines, still following the green posts. In less than a minute the GR waymarks point you up a SHORT-CUT to the left which soon brings you back out onto the main track. Turn left here until the waymarks indicate another SHORT-CUT to the left which quickly takes you up to a rather less transited track-cum-path. Turn left and then hairpin to the right. After about three minutes the green posts reappear on the relatively shady north side of Puig de les Agulles, just where Pyrenean bellflowers shine out from the scrub in June. From here, now on a decidedly narrow path, ten minutes' walking takes you up to a track on the top of the ridge; turn left and then left again shortly, to reach the rocky SUMMIT of **Puig de les Agulles** (552m/1810ft; **1h25min**). This is another perfect place to picnic in spring, amid hill-topping butterflies and screaming alpine swifts. *The Short walk turns back here.*

Follow the track down off the summit, heading southwest towards the distant *abocador* (the

vast rubbish dump which receives all of Barcelona's waste), then turn left almost immediately along another track. This drops you down (watch for the waymarked short-cuts) to the saddle of **Coll Sostrell** (**1h45min**). Continue straight on uphill along the track until the waymarks direct you along a narrow path on the right, into the scrub and all the way to the SUMMIT of **La Morella** (596m/1955ft; **2h15min**), the highest peak in this part of the Garraf.

Follow the continuation of the GR down off this summit to the southwest and turn left along a track for a couple of minutes, to a point where the red and white waymarks and the green posts part company. Follow the *paint waymarks* to the right through the scrub (more or less parallel to the track), passing first one and then another ruined FARM — a reminder that parts of the Garraf were once well cultivated — before reaching a circular grassy MEADOW overlooked by the twin RADAR STATIONS high up to your right (**2h30min**). This is an excellent area for seeing Thekla lark, tawny pipit, rock thrush, southern grey shrike and ortolan bunting in summer, and with luck one of the local Bonelli's eagles, as well as for observing migrating raptors and storks in September and October.

Head for the shade of the olive trees on the other side of the meadow, then follow the radar station road southwest downhill, *ignoring* the GR as it enters the scrub (to save your legs from being scratched). Ten minutes later you reach a wooden BARRIER, where you turn left down another, busier road (above all at weekends), now on a different branch of the GR-92 called the 'CAMI DE LES COSTES'. This takes

about 200m/yds you meet the GR-92 once again as it enters on a path from the right. Follow this track past the DOGS' HOME on your left and descend to skirt a vast QUARRY, also on your left. When you reach a small SADDLE (**3h25min**), look out for a SINGLE GREEN POST: this alerts you to go right along a track, which now begins a gentle, looping descent to the coast below. Once directly below the radio antennas on a peak above, the track narrows to a path then describes a couple of loops, before a quick wiggle heralds a long, straight eastward stretch, followed by an equally long westward return stretch.

On approaching the main road, a couple of sharp bends take you behind a house and then steeply up an unexpected 50m/yds ascent and out to a road. Follow this road to the left, with the main road just below on your left. After 200m/ yds the road makes a U-bend down to the left. Just before you meet the main road, turn right to pass through a TUNNEL under the road and then continue on through another TUNNEL beneath the railway line. Once out of the second tunnel, keep right for the final 300m/yds to the **Garraf RAILWAY STATION** (**3h50min**).

Above: on the path to the Puig de les Agulles and Glanville fritillary (Melitaea cinxia); right: Spanish gatekeeper (Pyronia bathsheba); below: knapweed fritillary (Melitaea phoebe)

you to **La Pleta** (**3h**), the information centre of the **Parc Natural del Garraf** (open daily from 10.00-15.00; (and Fax: 93 5970892; e-mail: p.garraf@ diba.es).
Continue downhill on the road. In five minutes, as the road swings left (**3h05min**), turn right* through a CHAIN and along an unsurfaced road. After

---

***Alternative descent**: At this point you can keep *left along the road* for a spectacular descent to the coast which may be a little easier for tired feet, and which might also turn up black wheatears in any month of the year and perhaps alpine accentors in winter. Follow the tarmac all the way down into the **Rat Penat** holiday home complex and then continue under the main coastal MOTORWAY to the BEACH (**4h**). From here, walk east along the beach for 2.5km/1.5m to reach the RAILWAY STATION of **Platja de Castelldefels** (**4h35min**).

Walk 2: BAIXADOR DE VALLVIDRERA • FONT GROGA • SANT MEDIR • CAN BORRELL • SANT CUGAT

Distance: 12km/7.5mi; 3h
Grade: easy; a shady, sometimes muddy walk along clearly marked paths, with an ascent of just 180m/590ft. Can be undertaken at any time of year. Some waymarking and signposting.
Equipment: boots or stout shoes, sunhat, cardigan, raingear, picnic, water
Access: 🚆 (FGC: Ferrocarrils de la Generalitat) from Plaça Catalunya station in Barcelona to Baixador de Vallvidrera (14min);

return to Barcelona from Sant Cugat (same 🚆, 23min). Trains run roughly every 5 minutes during the week and every 10 minutes at weekends. Or 🚌 to Baixador de Vallvidrera (2.5km northwest of the suburb of Vallvidrera via the BV1462, which can be picked up in Barcelona at the junction of the Ronda de Dalt and Via Augusta); return to your car by 🚆 from Sant Cugat (almost all trains stop at Baixador de Vallvidrera).

Hidden from the city of Barcelona, the north side of the Serra de Collserola is surprisingly verdant and well wooded and is thus a magnet for thousands of city-dwellers and, above all, mountain bikers, at weekends. Some of the best of the many signposted walks here follow the humid gullies which drain northwards, while good combinations of trains and buses turn linear walks, such as the one described, into round trips.

To start the walk, leave the station of **Baixador de Vallvidrera** under the sign reading 'PARC DE COLLSEROLA' and head up the large stone steps, disappearing straight ahead into the pines. You rise up to a road in a couple of minutes. Continue straight on to the **Centre d'Informació del Parc Natural de Collserola** (open daily from 09.30-15.00), 100m/yds ahead on the right (**5min**). Continue uphill from the centre and turn sharp left after two minutes along a broad UNSURFACED ROAD signposted 'ITINERARIS DE LA BUDELLERA'). This veers uphill and around to the right almost immediately, leaving behind a group of buildings and taking you deep into the pine forest. Keep uphill, ignoring a track off left after four minutes, and then branching down right four minutes later along a chained-off track (still marked 'ITINERARIS DE LA BUDELLERA'; **15min**). From here you enjoy splendid views of **El Tibidabo** (512m/1680ft) up to

the right, the mountain crowned by a monstrous neo-Gothic church and the Torre de Collserola, a communications tower built for the 1992 Olympic Games.
Cross the chain, dropping down into a humid GULLY, where two benches make a pleasant picnic spot. Follow the track up and out of the gully to reach, shortly, on a small ridge, another group of benches. Here, ignore the left and right turns and continue northeast as the track bends to the left. Drop down towards another well-wooded GULLY, and as track climbs up out of the gully, after a minute's walking, turn back sharp left on a path (now well marked as the GR-92) towards 'FONT D'EN CANET' (**25min**).
After about five minutes on this narrow path, passing through tall scrub composed predominantly of laurustinus, tree heath and the broom *Cytisus villosus*, you reach an enormous umbrella pine just metres/yards before you arrive at

the (often dry) spring of **Font d'en Canet**. Note the nearby cork oak with amazingly gnarled roots. From here, ignoring the path up to the right, continue *downhill* to the left. After crossing the gully, begin a steep climb on a path which takes you to a junction of paths in about five minutes (**35min**). Turn right uphill here and you will soon arrive at a HAIRPIN BEND on a broad unsurfaced road. Continue along the path (signposted 'COLL DE LA VINASSA') which brushes the hairpin at a tangent before disappearing back into the forest. A couple of minutes later, turn right onto a broad TRACK which takes you quickly to a CROSSROADS. Turn left, still following the GR-92 signs, and then turn right immediately along a path signposted 'LA MOLA' (**40min**). This path descends through well-preserved holm oak forest with superb views north to Sant Llorenç del Munt (Walk 4), although it is rather less than peaceful owing to the traffic noise from the road below. In just under ten minutes you arrive at the BARCELONA–EL TIBIDABO ROAD. Cross the road and turn left; at the road junction, continue straight on towards Barcelona. Cross the road again opposite the first house on your right and head straight into the forest along a path (signposted GR-92). This immediately bears right and runs parallel to the road, behind a group of buildings. On coming to a CAR PARK, bear left (*leaving* the GR) along a chained-off track which takes you into the area of **Font Groga**, the best-preserved part of Collserola (**55min**).
After five minutes, bear left at the first junction, entering attractive mixed woodland composed of large-leaved lime, London plane, holm oak and the rare Algerian

oak — this latter tree a semi-evergreen species with large, many-lobed leaves. Ignore the path off to the left just before you pass a PYLON on your right. You reach a WALL at a hairpin bend (**1h05min**), overlooking the verdant **Torrent de la Salamandra** (also known as **La Riera de Sant Medir**). Turn right downhill alongside the wall and, at the next bend (50m/yds), take an unmarked path on the right which leads to the permanent spring of

Font Groga (**1h10min**). This is an excellent picnic spot (see above), in the shade of tall holm oaks, although a sign warns that the water here is

Font Groga

not always potable. Retrace your steps to the main track (**1h15min**). Continue descending on this track and cross a STONE BRIDGE over the gully, almost immediately after which you turn right down a path. Running beneath fallen trees and through a humid forest full of sprays of soft shield-fern, this path leads to the bed of the *torrent*. Follow the stream bed downhill and then right along a path-cum-track. After five minutes, in a shady grove of London plane trees, crosses the *riera* and continues on the right bank to a CHAIN (**1h35min**). Negotiate this chain and continue downhill here to the left, ignoring a track off to your right, then a path down to the left and finally another track off to the right. Your track hairpins left to meet a broad unsurfaced road. Turn right here and follow the *riera* down past a

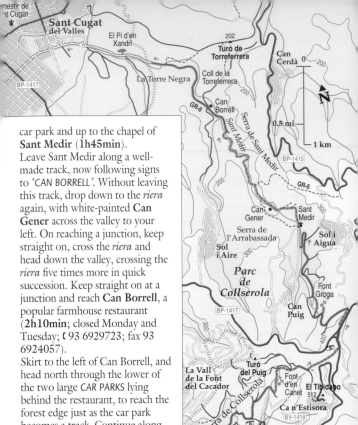

car park and up to the chapel of
Sant Medir (**1h45min**).
Leave Sant Medir along a well-
made track, now following signs
to 'CAN BORRELL'. Without leaving
this track, drop down to the *riera*
again, with white-painted **Can
Gener** across the valley to your
left. On reaching a junction, keep
straight on, cross the *riera* and
head down the valley, crossing the
riera five times more in quick
succession. Keep straight on at a
junction and reach **Can Borrell**, a
popular farmhouse restaurant
(**2h10min**; closed Monday and
Tuesday; ☎ 93 6929723; fax 93
6924057).
Skirt to the left of Can Borrell, and
head north through the lower of
the two large CAR PARKS lying
behind the restaurant, to reach the
forest edge just as the car park
becomes a track. Continue along
this track, keeping straight on
along an unsurfaced road which
joins from the right. Soon
(**2h35min**) Sant Cugat comes
into view, its distant skyline
dominated by a Benedictine abbey
— the Monestir de Sant Cugat,
built in mixed Romanesque and
Gothic styles and with a beautiful,
square, late 11th-century bell-
tower and 12-century cloister. A
little way ahead, **El Pi d'en
Xandri** — a huge umbrella pine
propped up by a number of
wooden supports — appears on
your right. Five minutes later you
cross the *riera* for the last time,
and climb to a roundabout on the
outskirts of **Sant Cugat**, a rapidly
expanding dormitory town. Go
straight on at this and the next
roundabout, then follow this main
street for about 15 minutes, until
you come face-to-face with an
attractive white house (just where
the main street veers left). Turn
right here along PASSEIG D'ÀNGEL
GUIMERÀ, to reach the RAILWAY
STATION (**3h**).

Walk 3: MONESTIR DE MONTSERRAT • PLA DELS OCELLS • SANT JERONI • PLA DE LES TARÀNTULES • SANT MIQUEL • MONESTIR DE MONTSERRAT

See also photographs on pages 14 and 20

Distance: 9km/5.6mi; 3h30min

Grade: moderate, with a total ascent of over 500m/1640ft on well-maintained concrete and dirt paths, including more than 1300 steps. An enjoyable walk at any time of year except high summer, *but should not be undertaken during or just after heavy rain, when the main gully can become a rushing torrent.*

Equipment: boots or stout shoes, sunhat, cardigan, raingear, picnic, water

Access: 🚆 (FGC) from the Plaça Espanya station in Barcelona (line R5) at 36min past the hour to Aeri de Montserrat, to link up with a cable car up to the Monestir de Montserrat (runs from 09.25 to 18.45) or the rack-and-pinion 🚌 from Monistrol; 🚌 from Plaça dels Països Catalans (next to Sants railway station in Barcelona) at 09.00, returning from the monastery at 18.00 (1h journey each way); 🚗 to Montserrat: park at the monastery entrance *(the car park fills up quickly at weekends and on public holidays).*

Short walk: Estació Superior (Pla de les Taràntules) — Sant Jeroni — Estació Superior. 6km/3.75mi; 1h20min. Easy, with just 166m/545ft of ascent; access, equipment and season as above. Take the rack-and-pinion 🚌 (runs every 20 minutes from 10.00-18.00) from the Monestir de Montserrat up to the Estació Superior at Pla de les Taràntules (a good picnic spot). Take the concrete path northeast along the main ridge to Sant Jeroni (40min), following the main walk in reverse; retrace your steps to return.

The Muntanya de Montserrat — also known as the 'mountain of the 100 summits' — is an implausible jumble of sheer conglomerate rock spires, left exposed once the erosive and, in this case, creative powers of the elements had removed the much softer overlying clays and marls. Crowds flock to the mountain (see Car tour 1), but few get far beyond the monastery, so that walkers — above all mid-week — will be able to get away from the crowds surprisingly quickly. Enjoy the flora: fissure-loving plants such as *Saxifraga catalaunica,* ramonda and Pyrenean bellflower — and the fauna: Spanish ibex, Bonelli's eagle and the chance of alpine accentor or wallcreeper in winter. This circular route takes you to the magnificent viewpoint of San Jeroni (1236m/4055ft), the highest point of the Montserrat Natural Park.

Start the walk at the **Monestir de Montserrat**: from the main car park, head for the far end of the principal monastery buildings. Here the first of many flights of STEPS leads you up to a sign indicating 'SAN JERONI' to the right.

Following the red and white paint waymarks of the GR-172, the path takes you immediately across a small BRIDGE over the main gully that you ascend during the first part of the walk. More steps lead you into an attractive mixed

Mediterranean forest characterised by holm oak, turpentine tree (adorned with curly, livid-pink galls in late summer), laurustinus, wild privet, common smilax and butcher's broom. Repeated flights of steps bring you to a new wooden BRIDGE, rebuilt after the floods in 2000, and then, after more steps and a stretch in the bottom of the gully itself, you arrive at a narrow pass between two massive boulders called the **Pas dels Francesos** (**15min**). Yet more STEPS eventually bring you to a small clearing, the **Pla de Santa Maria**, where the red and white GR markings head up to the right. At this point, however, you continue *straight ahead* along a flatter path, now marked by YELLOW ARROWS. Just after a short downhill section, a concrete PILLAR on your right engraved '**El Pla dels Ocells**' marks the path as you descend into and across the main GULLY and then back into the forest once more (**35min**). From here on, with the gully

Pas dels Francesos

always just to your right, the path leads you through shady enclaves of gallery forest, dominated by Montpellier and field maples, attractively red-leaved in autumn, and lined with martagon lilies in early summer. After about 10 minutes, you switch to the opposite side of the gully and then climb steeply up to your left, to meet the main CONCRETE PATH which contours just below the top of the ridge (**50min**). *This is your return route.*

Turn right here to enter a deep BREACH IN THE ROCKS — a veritable wind tunnel — a couple of minutes later, where the north-facing cliff is clothed with many of the typical fissure-loving plants of the area: clumps of the summer-flowering cinquefoil *Potentilla caulescens*, the regional endemic white-flowered saxifrage *Saxifraga catalaunica*, and *Paronychia kapela* with its strange papery bracts. Immediately afterwards, a wooden

67

Martagon lily (Lilium martagon)

sign points you towards 'SANT JERONI', and the path takes you up yet another long flight of STEPS into a flatter open area occupied by the **Ermita de Sant Jeroni** — a good shady picnic spot (**1h05min**).

Turn left here for the final ascent, passing first through woodland and then out into a bare rocky landscape for the final sets of steps to the viewpoint on the SUMMIT of **Sant Jeroni**. The views on a clear day as far as the sea and the whole of the eastern Pyrenees are phenomenal; gullies filled with large-leaved limes plunge down to the north, alpine swifts scythe the air overhead in summer, and the delicate, pink-flowered rock stork's-bill (*Erodium rupestre*) carpets the bare conglomerates (**1h20min**).

Retrace your steps back along the path to the 50min-point (**1h50min**), where you continue along the level, well-maintained path which runs all the way along the main ridge, keeping faithfully just to the east of the highest point. Here patches of forest alternate with clearings teeming with grass-leaved buttercup, common globularia and Pyrenean snakeshead in spring. After about 20 minutes, STEPS on the right lead up to a *mirador* for a quick view west, and from here onwards the ridge-top path offers a glorious panorama over the monastery below. After passing through two breaches in the rock in quick succession, you arrive rather

unexpectedly at the **Estació Superior** of the Sant Joan rack-and-pinion railway (**2h30min**), which doubles as an information point and field studies centre (*Escola de Natura*).

Here you can either descend via the railway or finish the circuit on foot. The main walk continues by crossing the **Pla de les Taràntules** — the esplanade behind the station — and taking the concrete track heading upwards and slightly to the left, signposted 'SANT MIQUEL 50MIN'. The track, upgraded in 2001 to provide better access for fire engines, hairpins up to the left and then crosses over to the southern, scrubby face of the mountain. Many forest fires have taken their toll here, and no trees remain to provide shade, the vegetation being dominated by holly oak, grey-leaved cistus and large clumps of the summer-flowering shrubby hare's-ear, with a ground layer including the delightful silver-leaved *Convolvulus lanuginosus*. On reaching a crossroads after 25 minutes of descent, turn left on the GR-172 and head down towards a large WATER TANK and thence to the chapel of **Sant Miquel** (**3h10min**). Just beyond the chapel, take a five minute there-and-back detour right along a concrete path to the **Creu de Sant Miquel**, a cross with stunning views over the monastery (an excellent picnic spot). Back on the main path, wind down past an eclectic series of monuments paying homage to — amongst others — St Francis of Assisi and the Catalan fire service. You drop quickly to the **Monestir de Montserrat** (**3h30min**).

Walk 4: COLL D'ESTENALLES • LA MOLA • LA BARATA • CAMÍ RAL • CASTELLSAPERA • COLL D'ESTENALLES

See also photograph page 18
Distance: 16km/10mi; 5h10min
Grade: moderate; a first ascent of 235m/770ft to the summit of La Mola, followed by a descent of 464m/1520ft and a second climb of 292m/960ft to the top of Castellsapera. The whole route follows clearly marked paths that coincide with routes signposted by the Sant Llorenç Natural Park or parts of the GR-5. *Avoid high summer.*
Equipment: boots or stout shoes, sunhat, cardigan, raingear, picnic, water
Access: 🚌 (RENFE, Sundays only) from the Estació de Sants or the Plaça de Catalunya station in Barcelona to Terrassa (four an hour; journey time 45min), then 🚐 to the Coll d'Estenalles (Timetables 2, 2a). Or 🚗 to the Coll d'Estenalles via the BV1221, the Terrassa–Talamanca road.
Short walk: Coll d'Estenalles — La Mola — Coll d'Estenalles. 12km/7.5mi; 3h 05min. Easy; with a total ascent/ descent of 235m/770ft; access, equipment and season as for the main walk. Follow the main walk to **La Mola** (**1h40min**) and return the same way.

The twin ridges of Sant Llorenç del Munt and the Serra d'Obac — both popular walking destinations for ramblers from Barcelona — are joined in a horseshoe shape at the Coll d'Estenalles (871m/2860ft), where there is an information centre open daily from 10.00-15.00. Both ridges are well wooded, with a mixture of holm oak and Aleppo, umbrella and Scots pines. Also characteristic of the area are myriad expanses of bare conglomerate rock, known locally as *codines* (singular *codina*), and numerous rounded conglomerate pinnacles, somewhat reminiscent of Montserrat. Our route takes in the two of the highest peaks in the area — La Mola (1107m/3630ft) and Castellsapera (939m/3080ft).

Start the walk at the **Coll d'Estenalles**: pick up the narrow road closed to traffic and signposted 'MONTCAU' and 'LA MOLA' that leads northeast from the information centre into the forest. You will notice the first of the small green METAL POSTS WITH ORANGE STICKERS that mark the route all the way to the summit of La Mola. The road starts off fairly steeply within a cool, shady holm oak forest, but then continues through a series of large *codines*. The denuded hump of Montcau (1056m/3465ft) is visible up to your left. A small saddle, the **Coll d'Eres**, makes a pleasant picnic spot, populated by mature holm oaks and a stone monument to the Catalan poet Joan Maragall (**20min**).

Giant fennel (Ferula communis)

Cliffs of Sant Llorenç

the left; instead continue straight on past an enormous UMBRELLA PINE on the right and down a steeper, rockier section. In five minutes you reach a JUNCTION of paths (**55min**). At this point turn left (marked with a green post) for a there-and-back detour of ten minutes along a path to **Els Òbits** (**1h**), a cliff housing a number of two-storey medieval cave dwellings. The views south to La Mola along this detour, plus shady spots under the oaks, make this an ideal place for a picnic.

Back on the main path, continue south. Shortly, next to another huge umbrella pine (**El Pi Tort**) and opposite a small metal POST (**1h05min**), *note the path leading down to the right which is the continuation of the main walk once you have climbed La Mola*. For the time being, continue straight on towards La Mola, enjoying views west to the Serra d'Obac and, as the path bends left, up to La Mola on your right. Large WHITE ARROWS appear; follow them down across a *codina* (a bare flat area), then descend steeply and

From the saddle continue straight on into the forest along a broad path which climbs gradually for 10 minutes, passing a green post and then veering right at a fork. After a further 10 minutes, as you round a bend, La Mola — crowned by its monastery — suddenly appears ahead in the distance. Head downhill from here. After almost 10 minutes, ignore a path off to

quickly to a SADDLE boasting a formidable rock pinnacle known as **El Morral del Drac** on the left. The needle-eye slit in this distinctive rock formation is said to resemble the muzzle of the legendary dragon killed on this spot by the Count of Barcelona (**1h20min**).

Continue straight across the saddle, past a metal post indicating 'LA MOLA', then take a small path running between forest on the right and bare rock on the left, the latter sporting clumps of *Saxifraga fragilis*. Barely a minute later you come to a short section of TRAIL which takes you quickly and steeply up to another area of bare rock, this time populated by *Saxifraga catalaunica*. Follow the green posts diagonally up and across the rocks to the base of a CLIFF and enter the forest. Cut back left immediately along a deep rocky gully (teeming with ramonda) and then climb up to an open area from where the rather braided path to the summit — momentarily out of sight — heads straight up and across a *codina* to the restored Romanesque church of **Sant Llorenç del Munt**, once part of a larger monastery, perched on the top of **La Mola** (**1h45min**). This 11th-century monastery, austere and built with rock hewn from the mountain of Sant Llorenç itself, is also open as a restaurant ((93 7435454; www.lamola.com). Birdwise, La Mola is renowned for a small group of alpine accentors which winter around the monastery, sometimes accompanied by the odd wallcreeper, as well as peregrine, alpine swift, crag martin, black redstart, raven and rock bunting. *(The Short walk turns back here.)*

Retrace your steps back to the 1h05min-point (**2h20min**) and turn left down the steep, narrow path you noted earlier, quickly encountering green and white, as well as green and red PAINT MARKS. Some 10 minutes later, cross a GULLY and a *codina*, before re-entering the forest almost immediately. Traverse the gully once again and continue through more open forest to the left of and above the gully, descending to a track running alongside the walls of the impressive buildings of **Can Pelags** (**2h40min**). Continue straight down alongside the walls, negotiating a CHAIN and then passing three different sets of GATES. Keep left at the first junction after 500m/yds, on an unsurfaced road. A field is on your right. Within 1km/0.6mi, you cross a dry river bed and then climb in 100m/yds to the ROAD at **La Barata** (**2h55min**).

Turn right along the road until, in 300m/yds, you pick up a PATH that climbs up into the forest on your left (next to a green POST with a *blue* marker). After two minutes you reach the **Camí Ral** ('Royal Path'), for many centuries the most important thoroughfare linking Barcelona and Manresa. Turn right here, crossing two gullies and ignoring a path up to the left just after the second. In quick succession, ignore two more paths off to the right, pass a green metal POST, and ignore a path angled back to the left. From this point the Camí Ral begins to climb and zigzag in earnest, reaching a *codina* in five minutes (**3h20min**); turn left here and head south into the forest for more zigzags. Next you cross a succession of *codines*, passing a small green post marked 'AL CASTELLSAPERA' and 'AL COLL DE TRES CREUS' in about 10 minutes, to reach the TOP OF THE RIDGE a couple of minutes later (**3h30min**).

At this point, turn right past a green POST, to emerge five minutes later at a large *codina* boasting spectacular views west to Montserrat (Walk 3). Head back into forest here, then cross another large *codina*. With Castellsapera looming above you, you enter the forest once more. Almost immediately you arrive at a junction of paths; turn right *(no sign, only a single yellow paint splodge on a rock)*, heading slightly uphill. Quickly crossing a small *codina* (**3h40min**), a small CAIRN on the far side marks a very steep path up to the summit of Castellsapera. *Fit* botanists may want to scramble up this rather precipitous route, which leads in five minutes to a metre-wide CLEFT IN THE ROCK, separating the two flat summits of **Castellsapera** (**3h45min**), which can be scaled with judicious use of the hands. The shadiest rocks here are covered with ramonda and *Saxifraga fragilis*, while the summit harbours plants typical of the *codines*: prickly juniper, the stork's-bill *Erodium glandulosum*, giant fennel and, in early spring, masses of diminutive rush-leaved jonquils, grape hyacinths and dipcadi, the latter resembling nothing so much as a brown 'bluebell'.

Back down on the path, continue north into the forest, reaching another *codina* and a JUNCTION of paths two minutes later. Turn right here, now following the GR-5, which is a well-marked route leading all the way to the Coll d'Estenalles. First you traverse an excellently preserved holm oak forest and in just under 10 minutes reach a junction of paths at the **Coll de Tres Creus**. At this point, keep left along a broad track. This leads to a short steep stretch of concreted track that bends left and then placidly heads north to the TOP OF THE RIDGE. From here, follow the GR-5 north along the ridge for 20 minutes, alternating between *codines* and forest, until you reach the small **Coll de Boix** (**4h30min**), at which point you follow the GR down to the right, off the ridge.

The GR rejoins the ridge-top 20 minutes later on reaching an unsurfaced road: keep right here, dropping down to the **Coll de Garganta** and then passing through a mature grove of holm oaks. Just 100m/yds further on, cross over a chain, leaving the chapel of **Sant Jaume** up to your right. As the track veers right, carry straight on along the GR, past an artificial POND, then go northeast down an unsurfaced road lined with planted cedars, back to the **Coll d'Estenalles** (**5h10min**).

Rush-leaved jonquils (Narcissus assoanus) *flourish on the stony* codines.

Walk 5: RIELLS DEL FAI • SANT MIQUEL DEL FAI • L'ULLAR • SANT PERE DE BERTÍ • CINGLES DE BERTÍ • SOT DEL BAC • EL FIGARÓ

See also photo on pages 16-17

Distance: 12km/7.5mi; 4h40min
Grade: moderate; the total ascent of 550m/1805ft is fairly gradual, although the final descent of almost 500m/1640ft to El Figaró includes some steep sections with loose pebbles. Most of the walk either follows the GR-5 or a local PR. Can be undertaken all year round, but is best floristically in spring and early summer.
Equipment: boots or stout shoes, sunhat, cardigan, raingear, picnic, water
Access: 🚌 from Barcelona to Riells del Fai (Timetables 3, 3a); 🚃 back to Barcelona from El Figaró (RENFE; 14.46, 16.24, 17.14, 17.52, 18.30, 19.39, 20.08, 21.38; journey time 1h)
Short walk: Riells del Fai — Sant Miquel del Fai — L'Ullar — Sant Miquel de Fai — Riells de Fai. 9km/5.6mi; 3h10min. Easy, with an ascent/descent of 400m/1319ft. Access: 🚌 to Riells del Fai or, on Sunday mornings,

to Sant Miquel del Fai (Timetable 3a; saves 3km/1.9mi; 40min). Or 🚗 to Riells del Fai (Car tour 1). Equipment and season as main walk. Follow the main walk to the 1h25min-point at the semi-abandoned farm of L'Ullar. From behind this farm, pick up the track heading left for 100m, before making a U-turn back above the house. Once you are just beyond the house, take a small unmarked path up left into the scrub, up through a small cleft in the bright white limesteone and then on up to a broad track (**1h35min**). Turn left on this track and, having ignored two left turns, continue as far as a junction just below El Soler de Bertí (**2h**). Turn left below this semi-abanoned farm and follow the track all the way down to the metalled road (**2h35min**) that climbs up from Sant Miquel del Fai. Turn left, back to Sant Miquel (**2h40min**), then pick up the path back down to Riells (**3h10min**).

On account of its spectacular waterfalls and cave systems, Sant Miquel del Fai (see Car tour 1) is a popular weekend destination for many Barcelonans, and is also an obligatory reference point for those wanting to explore the Cingles de Bertí, an impressive 15km-long calcareous escarpment with a rich flora. The Cingles are breached in just a few places by secretive paths leading down to the towns in the valley of the river Congost below.

The walk begins at the BUS TERMINUS in **Riells del Fai**, a village in the shadow of a long line of sheer cliffs. Head downhill along the broad unsurfaced road with GR-5 WAYMARKING, passing yellow, blue and green recycling bins. After 1km you reach a set of METAL GATES. Carry on through the gates and then head up to the right on a path between two wooden POSTS, from here

following a well-tended trail. This leads to a long set of STEPS which take you to the base of the cliffs at **Sant Miquel del Fai** (**40min**). At the top of the steps keep left and then continue to the right — unless you intend to visit Sant Miquel — through a narrow BREACH in the cliffs. Cross a STONE BRIDGE and turn right along a road towards the car park. After 100m/yds, on the other side of the stream, you will see a wooden signpost marking the GR-5 and indicating 'SANT PERE DE BERTI' (**45min**).

Cross or ford the small stream (usually dry) and follow the GR-5 steeply up into the scrub for five minutes, to emerge on a cliff top with superb views down over Sant Miquel del Fai. From here on the GR flattens out, passing through exuberant scrub — the result of repeated forest fires — characterised by an abundance of strawberry-trees and thus of the exquisite two-tailed pasha (whose larvae feast on the leaves of this species) in late summer. After ignoring a path up to the left and crossing a gully, begin a 20-minute stretch of path — accompanied by Dartford and subalpine warblers in the scrub and blue rock thrushes on the cliffs up to your left — which will take you to

Looking up to La Trona (below); the farm of L'Ullar (right); the waterfalls at Sant Miquel del Fai (far right)

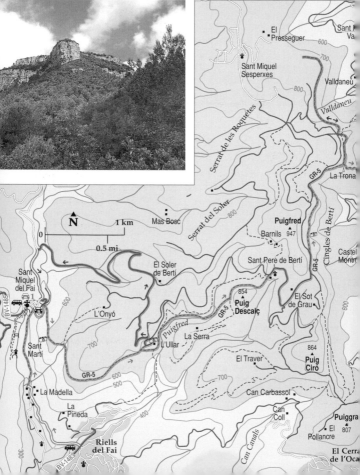

Having returned to the GR, continue north, soon passing a WOODEN SIGN (**1h30min**; *where the Short walk turns right*) and then entering a long stretch of path, always with the gully of **Torrent de Puigfred** just to your right. Forest fires have left a somewhat 'blasted' landscape in this section of the walk, with dead trees emerging from the scrub at weird angles, but even so, butterflies such as marbled skipper, Adonis, green-underside and Escher's blues and Glanville, knapweed and marsh fritillaries abound here. Eventually you descend to cross the gully and then head up and into a small enclave of well-preserved Scots pines. After a quick S-bend, the GR leaves the woods and reaches a track next to a solitary pine, where you turn right (**2h10min**).

Following this track, you skirt the small settlement of **Sant Pere de Bertí** (two houses and a church), passing between flower-rich verges, until after about 10 minutes you reach a CHAIN at a junction. Keep left until the tracks forks just as you reach a PYLON; take the right-hand fork here, but then immediately follow the GR straight on as it turns into a path running more or less parallel to the POWER LINES (**2h25min**). Almost immediately excellent views east to the Montseny (Walks 6 and 7) greet you, and the rock outcrop of La Trona — passed later in the walk — stands out ahead, somewhat detached from the main line of cliffs.

Before long, veer left along a track. Then, 300m/yds further on, follow a path down to the right through orchid-rich scrub: Bertoloni's, yellow, early spider and woodcock ophrys, and lesser butterfly, man and pyramidal orchids all bloom here in spring. When you come to a fork in the

within sight of an abandoned farm. While the GR passes *below* the farm, turn up left on the path marked with a red and white 'X' for a five-minute detour to the farm (**L'Ullar; 1h25min**), an excellent picnic spot.

woods, follow the GR down to the right, now immediately next to the edge of the La Trona cliffs (**2h 50min**). Keep to the edge of the cliff; after about 15 minutes (just after yellow and white PR WAYMARKS join your route) look for a metal sign on the right, at the edge of the wood, 'PR-C-33 EL FIGARÓ 1H45MIN'. (*But those enjoying the flora and views could continue north along the cliff-edge for another couple of kilometres before returning to this point.*) Follow this PR on a stony path-cum-trail which drops abruptly into the woods and then winds down to small SADDLE behind **La Trona** (June sees Pyrenean bellflower in bloom here most years).

The route then descends further into the forest along a walled-in cobbled trail

From top to bottom: woodcock orphys (Ophrys scolopax), *yellow orphys* (Ophrys lutea), *early spider orphys* (Ophrys sphegodes), *pyramidal orchid* (Anacamptis pyramidalis), *man orchid* (Aceras an-thropophorum)

which, always following the PR, reaches a fork in about 15 minutes (**3h30min**).

Bear right at the fork and shortly emerge on a wide FIRE-BREAK. Follow this southeast along the crest of a small ridge. At a small SADDLE, a cairn (but no paint) points you down right into the woods again along a narrow path. Cross over a track and pass through a GATE IN AN ELECTRIFIED FENCE, then begin a rather steep descent along a red-earth path which takes you out into the abandoned terraces of a RUINED FARM (**3h50min**). Continue downhill, crossing straight over a track (no paint marks) to descend along a well-trodden but slightly overgrown path. This quickly takes you across a gully and to an unexpectedly fine VIEWPOINT overlooking the cliffs of the **Sot del Bac**, the narrow valley that you will now follow all the way to El Figaró.

Wind steeply downhill on a rocky path, past a large graffiti-marred CAVE, and then descend more gently through well-preserved forest, with the traffic noise from the road in the valley bottom becoming increasingly louder. After about 25 minutes of descent, the PR heads rather too steeply down an eroded path to the left, so instead continue straight on and quickly reach an unsurfaced road. Turn left here and continue gently downhill, to eventually cross a RAILWAY LINE and pass a white-painted FACTORY on the outskirts of El Figaró (**4h30min**). Once past the factory, turn left and then right; head south along a mulberry-lined residential avenue to the **El Figaró** RAILWAY STATION (**4h40min**).

Walk 6: SANTA FE • FONT DEL BRIANÇÓ • LES AGUDES • TURÓ DE L'HOME • L'AVETOSA • FONT DE PASSAVENTS • SANTA FE

See also photographs on pages 22-23, 24

Distance: 9km/5.6mi; 3h50min
Grade: the total 565m/1855ft of ascent and descent makes this clearly waymarked walk fairly taxing. The mountains of the Montseny should be treated with respect, as low cloud at any time of year or even thick snow in winter are a distinct possibility, and ice patches will lie around for weeks on the high north-facing slopes. The ascent is marked by red paint, while the descent follows green posts placed by the Montseny park authorities.
Equipment: boots or stout shoes, sunhat, cardigan, raingear, compass, picnic, water; ski- or walking-poles in snowy conditions

Access: 🚌 or 🚐 (Saturday morning only) to Can Casades at Santa Fe (Timetable 4)
Short walk: Santa Fe (Can Casades) — Les Agudes — Santa Fe (Can Casades). 7km/4.4mi; 3h15min. Moderate, with the same ascent, but a much more direct descent than the main walk; access, equipment and season as above. Follow the main walk to the 1h45min-point at the summit of Les Agudes and return by the same route; this option avoids some of the potentially dangerous icy stretches on the north-facing slopes.

The Montseny Natural Park, visible from the centre of Barcelona on clear days, is a vast, verdant playground for the city's inhabitants. Unlike any other mountains described in this book, the upper slopes of this largely granite massif harbour a fully subalpine flora and fauna, including vast beech forests on the northern slopes and Europe's most southerly silver-firs. Unfortunately, the fact that a road reaches the summit of Turó de l'Home — which at 1706.4m (5597ft) is literally only centimetres higher than the neighbouring peak of Les Agudes — means that the area is somewhat less than deserted at weekends. Midweek throughout most of the year, however, you should have the place virtually to yourselves.

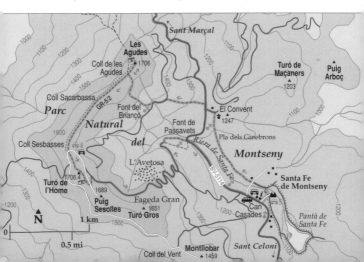

Start the walk at **Can Casades**, an information point of the Parc Natural del Montseny at **Santa Fe**, where you should head downhill past its entrance gates along a broad unsurfaced road to the architecturally challenged HOTEL SANTA FE. To the left of the hotel, pick up a track marked by a GREEN METAL POST WITH AN ORANGE SQUARE, which soon becomes a path and drops down some steps to two wooden bridges over the **Riera de Santa Fe**. Once across the river, turn left after 100m/yds along a track running parallel to the *riera*. This takes you to a crossroads of tracks at the entrance to the beech forest. Carry straight on here, passing a RUINED BRICK BUILDING on your right. Later, on reaching a T-junction opposite a patch of (planted) firs, turn left past a severe stone building known as EL CONVENT, to reach the road from Santa Fe at a sign reading 'COLL DE TÈ' a minute later (**30min**).

Turn right and walk along the road for 40m/yds, then take a track on the left. On the right, 40m/yds further on, look out for the RED PAINT that marks the path which will lead you all the way up through the beech forest to the ridge just below Les Agudes. Within 10 minutes cross straight over two tracks — just two of the many that have been cut into this part of the forest for extracting timber — and then turn left on a third track to start a straight uphill section of the route. Ignore a track entering from your left and continue straight on as your track becomes a path once more. Just after crossing over a gully, climb up and onto another track, continuing left for just 15m/yds before picking up the path again as it climbs up to the right (still well marked with red paint). After 500m/yds on this path, you reach

another track; turn left here, ignoring a track descending to your left. A couple of minutes later you reach the usually copious **Font del Briançó (1h10min)**. Just beyond this spring, your route

is a path that cuts up to the right off the track and quickly takes you to a junction of paths where 'AGUDES' is clearly painted in red on the beeches. Turn right here and then right again as you reach the end of another, this time overgrown, track. Next, turn right onto yet another track which curves around to the left — to where, some five minutes later, the red paint points you up a path to the left. This rises after just five minutes to the grassy **Coll de les Agudes (1h35min)** — carpeted with swathes of pheasant's-eye daffodils in May (photograph page 22). From here your rocky ascent path is obvious, and the reward from the SUMMIT of **Les Agudes** (1706m/5596ft; **1h45min**) is an immense panorama of the coast and the whole of the eastern Pyrenees, with an infinity of lesser ridges in the foreground.

Saxifraga genesiana *and the Font del Briançó (left)*

Having enjoyed the view, descend once more to the **Coll de les Agudes** and pick up the rocky ridge path heading southwest, clearly marked with GREEN METAL POSTS WITH BLUE SQUARES — indicating the GR-5/2. This route will take you all the way to the road below Turó de l'Home at Coll Sesbasses. Initially you keep to the north side of the ridge (beware ice patches in winter!), but cross to the south side once past the first major ROCK OUTCROP. Ignore a path heading downhill to the left from the ridge top and then, almost immediately, where the path splits, take the upper, right-hand option marked by GREEN METAL POSTS. This takes you directly to the road at **Coll Sesbasses** (**2h10min**). Alpine accentors frequent the area in winter, with other birds including black redstart and rock bunting all year round and possibly rock thrush in summer. Common wall lizards scamper everywhere, while the height of summer sees butterflies such as Queen of Spain fritillary, Piedmont ringlet, rock grayling and purple-shot copper on the wing.

From the road at the col take the obvious path up to the SUMMIT of **Turó de l'Home** (**2h15min**; photograph page 24), where a weather station has been permanently manned for over 50 years. Having admired the views once more, drop down to the southeast on a path leading to the road at the gates of the radar station on

Puig Sesolles, happily now in the process of being dismantled. Here, amid banks of wild tulips in May, pick up a track descending to the left off the road, marked by a METAL POST WITH A MAROON SQUARE: the first of the indicators that will accompany you on your return descent to Santa Fe.

After a short while, bear right and drop down towards a grassy SADDLE (**2h20min**), from where you should continue downhill to the right and into the beech forest, ignoring a path off to the left a little further on. As the track undulates downhill fairly gently, note the two ICE PITS in the trees below you on the left.

Eventually a METAL POST points you downhill to the left. Bear right a little further on (just where a gap in the forest gives you wonderful views back up to Les Agudes) and then veer left to begin a steepish section which brings you out into the top of **L'Avetosa** — the renowned silver-fir forest — amid a SCREE which harbours both *Saxifraga vayredana* and *S. genesiana*, the two saxifrages endemic to the Montseny (**2h35min**).

Just below the scree, turn right along the lower of the two tracks heading downhill. Then, following GREEN-POST waymarking, bear successively left, right at a fallen beech tree, and left again. Then ignore a path heading obliquely back to the right. From here bear right and then left, continuing steeply down to a gully, where you turn right. In a couple of minutes you reach the popular **Font de Passavets** (**3h05min**). Drop down from here immediately to the road, where you should turn right for the final 1.3km/0.8mi to **Santa Fe** and **Can Casades** (**3h50min**).

Distance: 10km/6.2mi; 3h55min (Alternative ascent adds 45min)
Grade: moderate-strenuous, with an ascent/descent of around 550m/1805ft. In winter thick snow may make route-finding difficult, and even in summer you should carry a compass in case the onset of poor weather reduces visibility, as it is important to pick up the correct spur when descending from the summit.
Equipment: boots or stout shoes, sunhat, warm weather clothing, raingear, compass, picnic, water
Access: 🚌 park at Collformic (Car tour 2 at 95km).

Unlike the neighbouring, road-accessed peak of Turó de l'Home (Walk 6), Matagalls (1697m/5566ft) is only ever conquered on foot and, as such, its summit is one of the more tranquil destinations in the Montseny. Even so, at weekends Matagalls is still fairly popular with ramblers, so we have opted to ascend from Collformic via one of the quieter, more verdant valleys that drain the Montseny to the north and then to approach the peak along a much less-frequented ridge; the descent follows the most popular route. Botanically, these northern slopes are renowned for their populations of *Saxifraga vayredana*, the sticky clumps of which are unique to rocks of the Montseny massif.

The walk starts from the car park at **Collformic** (1145m/3755ft) on the BV5301. Climb the steps on the northeast side of the pass, past a large MONUMENT commemorating the 1874 massacre of 110 Liberals — one of many that occurred during the cruel Carline wars that recurred during the 19th century; their bodies were subsequently left to rot in a nearby ice pit. Shortly you arrive at a broad track; cross straight over and pick up the very well-trodden GR-5/2 (marked by a GREEN METAL POST) as it heads steeply uphill through the sweet-smelling (in May) Pyrenean broom and into a small patch of sessile oak woodland. After a fairly strenuous climb, you encounter the original track again (**25min**); turn left here, leaving the GR, to head straight up towards the summit of Matagalls.

View to Matagalls, with Pyrenean broom (Cytisus purgans) *in the foreground*

Keep your eyes peeled for the woodlarks, red-backed shrikes and rock buntings which frequent these scrubby hillsides. At the first junction (**40min**), turn left by a GREEN METAL POST (where the main track bends up to the right towards the TV repeater station on Turó d'en Bessa). At this point, Matagalls is briefly visible up to the east, but it disappears again as soon as you cross over a small ridge, where you ignore a grassy track off left and drop down into the beechwoods which clothe the banks of the **Torrent de Rentadors**. Cross this stream at a pleasantly shady picnic spot, pass through a METAL GATE almost immediately, and then continue along the track. Just as the track

bends left over a gully and leaves the beechwoods (**1h05min**), take an obvious path up to the right* through the scrub to the grassy saddle of **Coll Saprunera** (**1h25min**; *the Alternative ascent rejoins the main walk here.*)

From the saddle the route simply follows one of a number of spurs which converge on the summit of Matagalls and consists of a gradual ascent to the southeast through a mosaic of pasture and rocky outcrops. After about 20 minutes, at the next grassy SADDLE, veer in a more easterly direction and pass through a large grassy swathe cut in the beech forest that creeps up from below on both sides of the ridge. Beyond the next grassy SADDLE the path becomes better

---

***Alternative ascent to the Coll Saprunera** (add 2km/1.25m and 45min to the main walk).*
This interesting but in part rather steep detour takes you to the Coll Saprunera via the ruins of the monastery of Sant Segimón, currently in the process of being converted into a restaurant and mountain refuge. From the 1h05min-point, where the main walk leaves the track and heads up right to Coll Saprunera, carry straight on along the track, past low rocky outcrops covered in forked spleenwort, thick-leaved stonecrop and *Saxifraga vayredana* — the latter known to locals, most appropriately, as the *herba de Sant Segimón* and best seen in flower in June.
After passing the gushing spring of **Font de Sant Miguel** on the right and re-entering the beech forest, you suddenly come upon the **Monestir de Sant Segimón** (**20min**). Walk through the MAIN ARCH and continue to the far end of the group of buildings, to a VIEWPOINT and a CAVE, the latter complete with a statue of Sant

Segimón himself. From just before the cave, take the very steep path that leads up to the right. After a first section in the open, take the right-hand fork as you enter the beech trees and continue steeply up to a rocky OUTCROP directly overlooking Sant Segimón, where the small chapel of **Sant Miquel de Barretons** perches uneasily on the edge of the cliff (**35min**). From the front door of the chapel, follow a narrow path southeast; almost immediately this begins to wind up across the rocks to your right. Now make sure that you keep to the *right* of the beech trees that here drift up from the thicker woods below. Circumnavigate the western edge of the rocky OUT-CROP above you and climb to a small grassy SADDLE, almost at the end of the long spur. You will follow this spur all the way to the summit of Matagalls. Head southeast along vague animal paths, keeping the top of the ridge immediately to your left, to arrive at the **Coll Saprunera** after 45min, where you rejoin the main walk at the 1h25min-point.

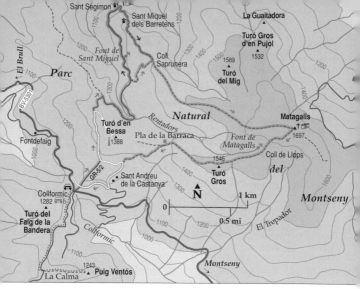

defined, heading up a more eroded and steeper section of the ridge to a rocky knoll. From here on the route is even clearer, as it leads over bare and rocky ground. The increasingly stunted common juniper bushes in this area provide refuge from grazing cattle for flowers such as early purple orchids and wild tulips. Soon you reach the SUMMIT of **Matagalls** (**2h25min**), topped by a huge metal cross. There is a marvellous view of the eastern Pyrenees and the foothills of the Montseny from here, stretching away towards the distant Costa Brava.

The descent to Collformic is obvious, although care must be taken to pick up the correct spur as you descend. From the summit head southwest over rough, animal-trodden paths, down to the small SADDLE known as the **Coll de Llops** (Wolf Saddle). From here a well-worn and fairly flat path continues west on the north side of the spur, skirting the base of **Turó Gros**, before beginning a relatively steep descent along braided paths which will take you to the level, grassy plateau of **Pla de la Barraca** (**3h20min**). A crater-like ICE PIT, once used to store natural ice for summer use, lies just to the north of the path here. Ignore the path which continues west from this plateau; take the rough and extremely eroded path southwest which drops steeply down through the scrub to a major track, where you turn left for a last easy stroll down to **Collformic** (**3h55min**).

The Monestir de Sant Segimón (Alternative ascent)

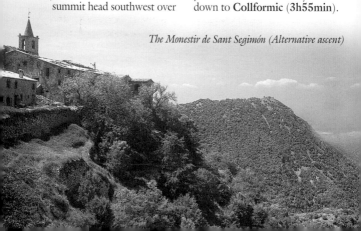

Walk 8: SANT ANIOL DE FINESTRES • FONT DELS SÒCALS • LES MEDES • PUIGSALLANÇA • SANTA MARIA DE FINESTRES • CASTELL DE FINESTRES • SANT ANIOL DE FINESTRES

Distance: 12.5km/7.8mi; 4h45min

Grade: quite long, with an ascent/descent of 627m/2055ft, including a few fairly steep sections. Red paint marks guide you for part of the route, and there are several potentially confusing turn-offs. Feasible in any season.

Equipment: boots or stout shoes, sunhat, cardigan, raingear, picnic, water

Access: 🚌 to Sant Aniol de Finestres. From Girona take the GI531, then GI530. From Olot take the C152, C63, GI531, then GI530. The GI530 ends at Sant Aniol. At the entrance to the village, turn right just after the bridge (wrongly signposted as the river Llémena), then turn left immediately (opposite a house).

There is a car park 80m along on the left. Or 🚌 to Sant Aniol from Girona (Timetable 5).

Short walk: Sant Aniol de Finestres — Font dels Sòcals — Serra de les Medes — Sant Aniol de Finestres. 6.5km/4mi; 2h20min. Moderate; an ascent of only 200m/650ft. Season, equipment and access as for the main walk. Follow the main walk to the 1h10min-point, then turn *left* along the track. Just after an S-bend (1h40min), turn left down a track which descends into thick woodland, then passes through a farmyard (2h). You reach the road just below Sant Aniol (2h10min). Turn right to the bridge at the entrance to the village, near the car park.

This walk explores the headwaters of the river Llémena, which rises in the Serra de Finestres — a ridge separating the humid beechwoods of the Garrotxa to the north from the more thermophilic holm oak forests that sweep south to Girona. The highest point of the walk is the 1027m/3370ft peak of Puigsallança, with its magnificent views north and east.

The walk begins at the CAR PARK in **Sant Aniol de Finistres**. Walk north along the unsurfaced road that leads over the Serra de Finestres towards Mieres. Cross a bridge over the **river Llémena** and turn left towards 'MIERES' and 'SANTA MARIA DE FINESTRES'. After 40m/yds, take note of a small path entering down a bank on the right: *this is your return route.* You pass a restored stone house on your left and, just two minutes later, turn left down a track. Almost immediately, you pass a house up to your right as you head towards the modern BOTTLING PLANT on the other side of the

Llémena. Drop down to a tributary stream of the Llémena (**15min**; usually dry), which you cross to continue uphill. The Llémena now runs in a small gorge below you to the left, and you pass a FARM. About 200m/yds further on, as the main track swings up to the right, keep straight ahead on a less well maintained track. Ignore two tracks off to the right as you begin to climb gently, then cross a gully and ignore two further overgrown tracks off to the right. 100m/yds after the third of these tracks, just before a sharp right-hand bend, take a small path off to the left

83

From top to bottom: Serra de Finestres; looking down to Santa Maria de Finestres, the path flanked by snapdragon (Antirrhinum majus)*; landscape with* Euphorbia nicaeensis *near Sant Aniol; Santa Maria de Finestres*

(CAIRN). This descends steeply to the banks of the Llémena (**40min**; often dry). The best place to cross the river is about 10m/yds upstream, where the continuation of the path is obvious on the far bank. Liberally decorated with ferns and lianas, this path begins to climb ever more steeply through the forest *between* the Llémena and a tributary stream, at first heading straight up and then zigzagging in tight bends. At a junction of paths (**55min**), turn left for some 200m/yds on a slightly overgrown path, to the **Font dels Sòcals**. The water gushes from the base of a boulder.

Retrace your steps just 50m/yds, then take a path up to the left. This takes you back onto the continuation of your original route and then climbs steeply to meet a broad track. Turn left here and quickly come to a much more frequently used track (**1h10min**). Turn right *(the Short walk turns left here)*, and keep straight ahead at the junction encountered almost immediately. Continue north, with the Llémena down below to your right. Ignoring a path off right and a track off left, you pass through a METAL GATE and come into pastureland — a pleasant picnic spot. Continue along the edge of these horse-grazed pastures to a group of ruined farm buildings known as **Les Planes de les Medes**. From here walk northwards along the track (in places just vehicle ruts) before curving down to the right to meet a TRIBUTARY of the Llémena. Cross this stream and continue up to the left, to a crossroads and a WIRE

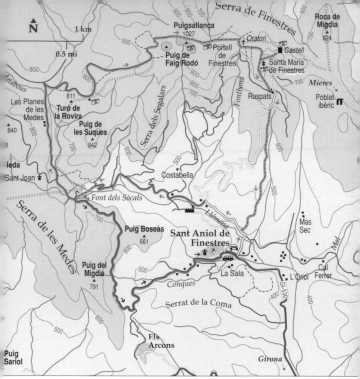

FENCE next to a large walnut tree. *Do not* cross the fence; instead head down to your right on a rough track and immediately ford the Llémena again (**1h25min**), then continue northeast, with the river to your left.

After just 100m/yds you come across the first RED PAINT MARKS, indicating a short-cut to the right, straight up into the beechwoods. While these will help guide you to the summit of Puigsallança, it is simpler here to *continue straight on along the track*. The track soon winds up to the right, through beech and then holm oak woods, to a RUINED FARM (**1h35min**) in the middle of a small, grazed saddle with fine views south. Continue straight uphill on the same track (noting after about 150m/yds the faint red paint marks on your right indicating the short-cut). The track describes a broad right-hand curve around a wooded summit, then re-enters the beech-

woods and begins a long, direct climb northeast and then east over bare rock.

Ten minutes later you reach a small CLEARING (**2h05min**). Here, as the track swings left into the beech forest, red arrows on the track point *both* left and straight on along a path. *Ignore* this latter path (despite the wooden sign reading 'Finestres'); instead, keep left. Shortly, when the track divides, bear up to the right. Begin to wind uphill on a slightly over-grown track and then path, to the left of the two magnificent beeches which lie just below the wooded summit of **Puig de Faig Rodó**. Drop down slightly from here, now on a track, to a small over-grown saddle, marked by a STANDING STONE. Continue northeast along a path which climbs to the top of the ridge (RED PAINT MARKS all the way) and then onto the SUMMIT of **Puigsallança** (**2h25min**). From here you enjoy

85

stunning views of the Costa Brava, the Canigó (a high, isolated peak in the French Pyrenees) and the mountains of the Alta Garrotxa and the village of Santa Pau to the north.

Follow the path southeast off the summit along the ridge top for five minutes, before dropping sharply down into the beech forest past a rock where 'AL PUIGSALLANÇA' is painted in red. Taking care here to follow the rather faded red paint marks (especially if fallen leaves have obscured the path), wind downhill through the beeches and then contour along the south side of the ridge amid holm oaks. Eventually you drop down through a group of large rocks to suddenly obtain excellent views southwards (**2h45min**). Wind down from here on the north side of the ridge to a large breach in the cliffs called **El Portell de Finestres**, from where you should continue following the red paint on the *north* side of the ridge. Some 40m/yds further on the path divides; keep right, uphill, twice in quick succession — the second time on a trail-like path which leads back up to the ridge-top and to the **Oratori de Finestres** (**2h55min**), a small shrine dedicated to Sant Antoni. Continue now on the south side of the ridge, ignoring two paths down to the right in quick succession, to reach **Santa Maria de Finestres** (**3h05min**). This group of buildings includes a small shelter and a Romanesque church (rebuilt in the 18th century after the destruction wreaked by the 1427 earthquake).

To visit the Castell de Finestres from here, turn up the flight of steps on your left as you enter the group of buildings and then follow vague red paint northeast over bare rock and into the holm oak forest. Keeping northeast and

uphill, pass through another breach in the cliff, onto the north side of the ridge. From here steps lead you up to the base of the castle. Scramble over the bare rocks — carpeted in May with rock soapwort, *Saxifraga fragilis*, kidney vetch and snapdragon. From the scant ruins of the **Castell de Finestres** (**3h25min**) yet more magnificent views can be enjoyed.

Retrace your steps to Santa Maria (**3h40min**) and head through the ARCH on the right of the church to pick up the well-trodden path winding down over the bare rock, following faint red paint-marks (reinforced by the occasional CAIRN) all the way. Keep downhill and southeast at all junctions. When you reach a track (**3h50min**), turn left, immediately passing the half-hidden ruined farm of **Raspats** on your right. From here drop down to a broad unsurfaced road, where you turn right and begin to descend once more. Look out ere for monkey ids (*Orchis simia*; see in May).

After 500m/yds, where this track swings right, cross through an ELECTRIFIED FENCE and follow another track bearing left (**4h**). After just 40m/yds, turn right into the woods down a narrow path — the centuries-old route to Santa Maria. This drops steadily southwards, most of the time over bare rock. After a short flat stretch, you enter a clearing where CAIRNS indicate your path back down into the forest. This returns you to the bank mentioned at the beginning of the walk, from where it is but a short stroll left along the unsurfaced road back to the CAR PARK in **Sant Aniol de Finestres** (**4h45min**).

Walk 9: COLL DE BRACONS • FONT TORNADISSA • RASOS DE MANTER • PUIGSACALM • RASOS DE MANTER • FONT TORNADISSA • COLL DE BRACONS

See also photograph pages 4-5
Distance: 8km/5mi; 2h30min
Grade: easy, with an ascent and descent of just 255m/835ft along a well-trodden path waymarked with red and blue paint. Possibility of snow in winter.
Equipment: boots or stout shoes,

sunhat, cardigan, raingear, picnic, water
Access: 🚌 to the Coll de Bracons on the road between Olot and Vic. *Note:* a major trunk road, with a tunnel under the Coll de Bracons, will change access in the near future.

Among Catalan walkers, Puigsacalm (1515m/4970ft) and neighbouring Puig dels Llops (1486m/4875ft) are two of the best-loved peaks, as the gentle ascent through delightful beech woodland and across rolling pastures is rewarded by a broad panorama of northeastern Catalonia and the eastern Pyrenees from the summit. In spring the grassy uplands are carpeted with drifts of spring and trumpet gentians, which are replaced in summer by a few tall spikes of great yellow gentians, while in September the pastures are coloured with autumn crocuses and the occasional ciliate gentian. All of these species are highly toxic to grazing livestock, hence their ability to thrive in such heavily grazed habitats, but great yellow gentian roots were once much collected by the local people on account of their medicinal and tonic properties (this is now prohibited by law, as wild populations were suffering).

The walk begins at the **Coll de Bracons,** on the narrow road that links the peaceful Vall d'en Bas in the Garrotxa with the Plana de Vic. The one and only complication of the walk occurs in the first five metres/yards! You have to half-scramble up the bank on the north side of the pass (following RED AND BLUE PAINT-MARKS) to reach your narrow, but very obvious path. This takes you into the mixed beech and downy oak woodland, here accompanied by common juniper, hazel, box, holly and whitebeam. After a short stretch of paved trail, the path begins to climb and 'braid', where people have taken short cuts; we advise you, however, always to follow the rather faded red and blue paint marks, keeping left on three occasions where eroded paths lead straight upwards.

Eventually the path levels out and, after another short section of trail, flat stretches alternate with short ascents. Here you will see spring flowers similar to those mentioned in Walk 11 — plus clumps of Lent-lilies. Just over 10 minutes

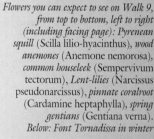

Flowers you can expect to see on Walk 9, from top to bottom, left to right (including facing page): Pyrenean squill (Scilla lilio-hyacinthus), wood anemones (Anemone nemorosa), common houseleek (Sempervivum tectorum), Lent-lilies (Narcissus pseudonarcissus), pinnate coralroot (Cardamine heptaphylla), spring gentians (Gentiana verna). Below: Font Tornadissa in winter

later, immediately after a small path cuts down to the left, your route veers steeply up to the right past an enormous, half-fallen beech daubed with blue and red paint. It then zigzags up to a crossroads of paths at the small pass of **Collada de Sant Bartomeu** (**35min**), which is little more than a cleft in the rock. Pass through the wire and turn right, walking over the word 'PUIGSACALM' painted on the ground, then fork downhill almost immediately onto the lower and broader of two paths. Still following the red and blue waymarks, contour in and out of a series of gullies until the path begins to climb, at first gradually but then zigzagging more steeply. Eventually the path starts to descend once more and later widens out into a track. You skirt a gully and a couple of minutes later arrive at a sign pointing you up to the right, to 'PUIGSACALM' and 'FONT TORNADISSA'. On reaching the permanent — and extremely welcome on a hot day — spring of **Font Tornadissa**, head up to the north through an obvious CLEARING in the forest, towards the skyline. You emerge on the well-grazed pastures of the MAIN RIDGE (**1h**). From here there are superb views to the northwest towards Puig de Miralles (1435m/4710ft) and south to the beech-covered peak of Puig de les Civaderes (1446m/4745ft). Puigsacalm, however, still lies hidden to the east.

Continue east uphill along the top of the ridge, which curves gently to the right, until you reach a white SIGN (**1h10min**) at the edge of the beechwoods marked 'Rasos de Manter' and indicating Puigsacalm to the right. Follow the FENCE to the right and uphill along the edge of the beech forest for five minutes, until the red and blue paint marks usher you down to the left through a wooden GATE. You briefly enter the forest, then head back into the open once more, now with Puigsacalm in view straight ahead. A further stretch through pastures, accompanied by northerly views, takes you back into the beech where, after a short climb, you reach a FIRST-AID BOX and a sign marked 'PUIGSACALM'.

Here, either ascend steeply to the right to the SUMMIT of **Puigsacalm** (**1h30min**), or continue left towards 'SANTA MAGDALENA, OLLETES, SANT-PRIVAT' and on to the SUMMIT of **Puig dels Llops** (**1h45min**). Both are excellent vantage points for short-toed eagles, hovering with deep wing-beats, as they hunt their reptilian prey over the surrounding countryside. Choughs and ravens circle the peaks, and tree pipits and black redstarts are closer at hand. Flowerwise, the high pastures are packed with orchids in May and June (elder-flowered and black vanilla orchids, respectively) and the cliffs below the summits sport Pyrenean saxifrage and other rock-loving plants.

The path down from Puig dels Llops to Santa Magdalena is rather steep (see the map for Walk 10) and treacherous in rain, so return along the same route to the **Coll de Bracons** (**2h30min**).

Walk 10: SANT PRIVAT D'EN BAS • MARE DE DÉU DE LES OLLETES • SANTA MAGDALENA DEL MONT • (PUIG CORNELI) • SALT DE SALLENT • SANT PRIVAT D'EN BAS

See also photograph pages 4-5
Distance: 10km/6.2mi; 4h
Grade: moderate-strenuous, with an ascent of 680m/2230ft, all in the first section of the walk, and a rather vertiginous descent from Salt de Sallent; for reasonably experienced walkers only. Possible any time of year, but best avoided after heavy rain.
Equipment: boots or stout shoes, sunhat, cardigan, raingear, picnic, water
Access: 🚌 to Sant Privat d'en Bas. From Olot take the C152 south. At Les Preses turn right on the GIP5226. At the entrance to Sant Privat turn left up an unsurfaced road signposted to (amongst other places) 'Puigsacalm'. After 1km head down to your right and park at a popular picnic site amid the pines (10.5km from Olot).
Alternative walk: El Camí dels Matxos. 8km/5mi; 2h30min. Moderate-difficult, with an ascent and descent of 450m/1476ft. Season, equipment and access as for main walk. **El Camí dels Matxos** is one of the best-preserved medieval trails in Catalonia and an impressive but steep route up to the Salt de

Sallent. From the picnic site, walk back to the unsurfaced road and turn right, ignoring the left turn towards Can Turó. Instead you quickly come to a metal BARRIER and a SIGN (**5min**) pointing you either left up a narrow path to 'Salt de Sallent pel Camí dels Matxos' — an extremely steep short-cut which is *not* recommended — or straight on to 'SALT DE SALLENT PER LES ESCALES'. Continue straight on, then turn *left* up a track (**10min**; where a wooden sign indicating 'Salt de Sallent' points down to the right). Keep straight on at a crossroads of tracks and then hairpin left along a gentle uphill track through butterfly-rich (for example, Duke of Burgundy in June and high brown fritillaries in July) open forest and scrub to another hairpin, which is where the aforementioned steep short-cut rejoins your route (**25min**). Follow the track as it winds uphill until it reduces to a path and almost immediately turns into a centuries-old TRAIL; it is here that you commence the spectacular journey up to the top of the cliffs far above. Cross a boulder-strewn

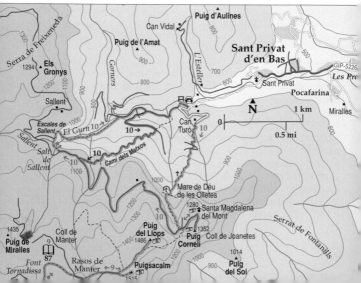

Santa Magdalena (2h on the main walk route) is an ideal picnic spot.

GULLY (**55min**) and continue along the far side for three minutes; now the trail heads away from the gully, rounds a bend and drops a little before beginning its giddy zigzag ascent. Veer left around a bend, cross a rockfall in five minutes, and then ignore a path, marked by a cairn, cutting back up to your left. Continue straight on — now almost on the flat — to cross a stream and join the MAIN WALK AT THE 2H50MIN-POINT (**1h20min**). From here follow the main walk to the **Salt de Sallent** and then back down to the car park (**2h30min**).

T hree paths lead from the picnic site just beyond Sant Privat d'en Bas up to the spectacular waterfall of Salt de Sallent. The main walk follows the two longer alternatives (one up and one down). The wonderful medieval paved trail known as the Camí dels Matxos (Mules' Trail) is described in the Alternative walk as the ascent route. Whichever option you follow, all possess the necessary ingredients of a great walk: thick forests, towering cliffs, an immense waterfall, stunning views, sun and shade, and many similar plants to those described in Walk 11, although here they flower a couple of weeks later.

The walk begins at the PICNIC SITE 1km beyond **Sant Privat d'en Bas**. Walk back to the unsurfaced road and turn right up the hill, then turn left and follow signs to 'CAN TURÓ' and 'PUIGSACALM'. Having reached the restaurant of CAN TURÓ (we don't recommend that you sample its excellent food *before* the climb!), head through an ARCHWAY on the left of the building and pass some green BENCHES and stone TABLES. Pick up a narrow, stone-flagged path which enters the forest next to a WOODEN INDICATOR POST (**15min**). Shortly, ignore a path off to the left and start to climb in earnest — always following the wooden posts — through a thick mixed forest of downy oak, *Acer granatense*, sweet chestnut, wild cherry, hazel and yew.
After a steep and fairly direct ascent you arrive at a wider path-cum-track crossing yours (**25min**),

91

where you turn left, then right to short-cut a right-hand hairpin bend. Then go left again immediately, this time up a steep path into the forest. This fairly narrow path eventually becomes a little less distinct on entering the pure beech and box forest, especially when the ground is covered by dead leaves, but a few red paint marks will help you find your way as you meander upwards. *(Please avoid the direct vertical short-cuts, as they cause erosion.)* After about 20 minutes, a small METAL CROSS set on a rock on your right (**50min**) is a sign that you are on the right path. At a T-junction with a sign indicating 'LES OLLETES', turn right. As the path bears right and levels out, you suddenly approach the foot of a huge CLIFF covered with clumps of ramonda and then come to an esplanade in front of a GATED CAVE containing a statute of **La Mare de Déu de les Olletes** (Mother of God of the Small Saucepans!; **1h05min**).

From the esplanade, ignore the path leading down to a spring; instead, head left uphill past a beech tree marked with a large RED ARROW. Although initially on the flat, this path quickly crosses a gully before starting to zigzag its way up a trail between two steep gullies, with the cliffs towering
92

above you to the left. After more than 30 minutes of meanders, the path passes diagonally across a large smooth rock, topped by a boulder which partially obstructs the path. Pass through a small cleft just beyond the boulder, for a more level final section up to a broad track (**1h55min**). Turn left on this track towards 'SANTA MAGDALENA', ignoring both the downhill track just to the left and the path to the right towards 'Puigsacalm' (Walk 9). The track leads you into the pastures surrounding the restored chapel of **Santa Magdalena** (1280m/ 4200ft; **2h**). The marvellous views here make this an ideal picnic spot. For those with energy to spare, an option is to ascend **Puig Corneli** for even better views to the south and east (35 minutes return; *not* included in main walk timings); the path lies directly behind and to the south of the chapel.

Retrace your steps from Santa Magdalena to the JUNCTION at the 1h55min-point and carry on northwest down the broad but rather rough track. After 25 minutes, hairpin down to the right and then head back to the left, to pass through the upper part of a large expanse of pasture with a small pantile-roofed HUT in its centre (**2h25min**). This pasture is

Opposite: view from near the Salt de Sallent; right: La Mare de Déu de les Olletes and golden-ringed dragonfly (Cordulegaster boltonii); *below: elder-flowered orchid* (Dactylorhiza sambucina)

studded with elder-flowered orchids in May. Re-enter the forest along the continuation of the track you've been following, in 25 minutes coming to a SIGNPOST indicating 'Sant Privat 1h' (**2h50min**; *the Alternative walk joins the main route here*). Continue straight on towards the Salt de Sallent, turning right into the woods five minutes later (as indicated by another SIGNPOST). Cross a first stream and then come to the **Riera de Sallent**, just at the point where it disappears over the precipice to your right to become the **Salt de Sallent**; a barbed-wire FENCE prevents you from getting too close to the edge of the cliff. Carry on across the *riera* and then follow the path alongside the FENCE and cliff-edge, to a rusty red GATE next to a signpost indicating the path down to 'SANT PRIVAT' (**3h05min**) — your onward route.

This descent, down the **Escales de Sallent**, can be rather difficult to negotiate, especially if heavy rain has turned the path into a stream; in two places ROPES provide additional hand-holds on short rock faces. About five minutes from the top, a sudden clearing gives you the best view back up to the waterfall, after which you arrive at the two roped sections. The final stretch of the descent consists of many semi-natural steps, eventually leading you to the river and the base of the cliffs (**3h25min**).

Ford the river and pick up a path heading east along the base of the cliffs, which is soon regularly marked with WOODEN POSTS. *Now* look back up to see what you've just climbed down! After 10 minutes you pass an enormous gnarled beech tree on your left, followed shortly by another beech with a red mark — indicating that you should follow the steepish path downhill to the left and ignore the right-hand option. From here WOODEN POSTS appear at intervals, and after about 15 minutes the path reaches a broad track (**3h50min**). Turn right here and come to another track (*where the Alternative walk diverged*): keep left and head downhill to a CATTLE GRID and a SIGNPOST indicating the Camí dels Matxos up to your right. Skirt the METAL BARRIER a few metres ahead, after which two large STONES on the left soon indicate the path back down to the picnic site and CAR PARK near **Sant Privat d'en Bas** (**4h**).

93

Walk 11: OLOT (PARC NOU) • LA MOIXINA • FAGEDA D'EN JORDÀ • SANT MARTÍ DEL CORB • SANT MIQUEL DEL CORB • VOLCÀ DEL RACÓ • LA MOIXINA • OLOT (PARC NOU)

Distance: 15km/9.3mi; 3h40min
Grade: easy underfoot, with an ascent/descent of just 180m/590ft, although fairly long. For the most part the walk follows PNZVG (see below) walks 3, 9 and 12, as well as a small section of the GR-2. It can be undertaken all year round, although spring is undoubtedly best for the flora.
Equipment: boots or stout shoes, sunhat, cardigan, raingear, picnic, water
Access: 🚌 to Olot, then follow signs through the town to the Museu/Casal dels Volcans and park there. 🚐 to Olot (Timetables 6, 6a, 7, 7a)
Short walk: Olot (Parc Nou) — La Moixina — Can Serra — Fageda d'en Jordà — Can Serra — La Moixina — Olot (Parc Nou). 9.5km/6mi; 2h30min. Easy; access, equipment and season as above. Follow the main walk as far as the 55min-point, where you turn left towards 'APARCAMENT DE LA FAGEDA D'EN JORDÀ' at Can Serra. Ignore a left turn towards some houses and then pass under the Olot/Santa Pau road about five minutes later. Quickly reaching a sign for 'SENDER 1' (see Walk 12), turn right up the steps to the information point of **Can Serra** (**1h05min**). From here follow Short walk for motorists 🚗7 on page 27, which makes a circuit back to Can Serra (**1h25min**). Then retrace your steps to **Parc Nou** in **Olot** (**2h30min**).

The Parc Natural de la Zona Volcànica de la Garrotxa (PNZVG), to the southeast of Olot, protects the Iberian Peninsula's largest and youngest volcanic landscape, dotted with extinct cones and lava flows which, for the most part, are clothed with extensive beech and oak forests. Highlights include an extremely rich spring ground flora and diverse faunal communities, with more than 100 species of butterfly having been recorded here. The route described gives you a good introduction to the deciduous forests and their botanical riches, and can also link up with Walk 12 for a circuit of the most outstanding geological features of the park.

Start the walk in **Olot**, at the botanical gardens of **Parc Nou** in the southwestern part of the town. Both an INFORMATION POINT for the PNZVG and the excellent **Museu dels Volcans** are located here in **El Casal dels Volcans** (Av. Sta. Coloma s/n, 17800 Olot; ☎ 972 266202; Fax 972 266012; open 09.00-14.00, 16.00-19.00). Behind this elegant building you will find a sign marked 'SENDER 3' and indicating various destinations. Follow the direction 'PARATGES DE LA MOIXINA', going

through a METAL GATE and heading right along an unsurfaced road. Keep straight on at the first junction (no sign) and then turn left 50m/yds further on (SIGN), along a raised grassy track with allotments on the either side. Pass a white house on your right and then turn left at a SIGN (**10min**), to follow a busy road towards a ROUNDABOUT. After 100m/yds, cross the road (care!) and follow signs for SENDER 3 between walls of volcanic rock that zealously guard more carefully tended

allotments. Shortly, turn right along a small road.

After passing a last group of houses on the right, this road enters the humid pedunculate oakwoods of **La Moixina** (a delightful place for a picnic), which in March are coloured by lesser celandine, both wood and yellow anemones, large bittercress and the lungwort *Pulmonaria affinis*. Turn left at a T-junction of roads (**20min**) and continue to the left at a STONE HOUSE. (Note that the walk will end along the track that enters here on your right.) After about 500m/yds you reach a group of houses on your left. Beyond the last house, and next to a group of blue, green and yellow RECYCLING BINS, cut diagonally right along a vague path across a field — towards a huge WHITE CROSS.

Meeting another road on the far side of the cross (**30min**), turn right uphill. This small road winds

Sant Martí del Corb

past a farm on the right and two houses on the left. Ignore all turn-offs until the tarmac changes to CONCRETE (**50min**). Some 30m/yds further on, bear left towards the woods, as signposted, and continue on a sunken track (ignoring a turn to the left). You will come to a crossroads (*not shown on the free maps given out by the park*). Continue straight ahead into the renowned beechwood known as the **Fageda d'en Jordà** (albeit with numerous sweet

95

chestnuts initially). At the first junction of tracks (**1h**), bear right following signs to 'FAGEDA D'EN JORDÀ'. *(But turn left for the Short walk or to link up with Walk 12.)* Ignore two turns to the right (just as you pass a house on your right) and then two tracks off to the left. At a crossroads of tracks continue straight ahead. At the point where a track joins from behind and to the left, explore the surrounding woodland for May-flowering species such as bastard balm, yellow archangel, angular Solomon's seal, twayblade, white and sword-leaved helleborines and bird's-nest orchid.

A couple of minutes later you reach the first of a group of buildings known as **Can Jordà** (**1h15min**) — the PNZVG documentation centre — where you should turn sharp right, following signs indicating the GR-2 and PNZVG walk 12 to 'SANT MARTI DEL CORB'.

On coming to a concreted section of track, pass below a house and then, once you have re-entered the woods, ignore two right turns in quick succession. Leave two houses (CAN PLANISSAS and LA PORTUGUESA) to your left. A little further on, ignore the left turn signposted 'Can Vidal' and 'Can Roure' and, now on concrete again, drop down to reach a farm and a road. Turn right here and follow the tarmac for about five minutes, until you come to a track off to the left signposted 'ELS CAMPS' and 'SANT MARTÍ DEL CORB' (**1h40min**): this is your onward route.

Having turned left, you pass on your right the twin buildings of **Els Camps** within 300m/yds, from where you continue uphill along the same track, to reach the diminutive but charming Romanesque church shown on page 95 — **Sant Martí del Corb** (**2h**), with a permanent SPRING. Look around here for fire sala-manders and, in March, veritable carpets of hepatica, wood ane-mone, pinnate coralroot, purple gromwell and Pyrenean squill. Walk in front of the church, following the track to the farm of **L'Antiga**, surrounded by huge spruces (**2h05min**). From here pick up a track heading left, signposted 'SANT MIQUEL', to continue gently uphill, with orchards and farm buildings below to your right. Having passed through two ELECTRIFIED FENCES, you reach **Sant Miquel del Corb** (**2h15min**), a second Roman-esque delight.

From here continue along the track passing to the right of Sant Miquel. This climbs quickly, turns into a path and then enters a small clearing. Keep right and climb quickly to a small SADDLE, from where you descend into the beechwoods. At a fork in a couple of minutes, keep right again, slightly downhill. After five more minutes the track narrows to a path and crosses a damp gully, full of hart's-tongue, green hellebore, tuberous comfrey and ramsons. Shortly the often-dry **Font del Racó** appears on your left, just before you enter a shady holm oak forest. The path then continues to the modern farm of **Mas El Racó**, with the circular crater of the **Volcà del Racó** in front of you (**2h35min**).

Turn left past the farm to circum-navigate *half* of the crater. Then, as the path becomes a track, veer northeast and descend into the beech forest. Bear left on a path marked by a POST WITH A BLUE DIAMOND and then, where the path joins a track, continue downhill to the right. Cut down left again on a rather indistinct path (again

marked by a BLUE DIAMOND); this leads in two minutes to a RUINED FARM and a cross-path — the GR-2. Turn right here and reach a flimsy GATE three minutes later. Walk through this gate into a meadow and take a path down to the left, past a large oak, shortly reaching a road. Follow the road to the left for 500m/yds, then turn right along another road signposted 'VEINAT DE POCAFARINA' and 'BOSC DE TOSCA' (**2h55min**).

After two minutes turn right along a track signposted 'BOSC DE TOSCA', then go left 200m/yds further on at a BLUE DIAMOND marker (opposite a low, rambling house). Follow this track between walls of volcanic stone, ignoring all turn-offs, until you reach a broader track next to a large STABLES. Turn left and then imme-diately left again onto a road. At a signpost, 'LA MOIXINA', turn right and then immediately left downhill on a track. After ten minutes this track, which soon becomes a trail, takes you back to the 20min-point of this walk (**3h 20min**). Retrace your steps via **La Moixina** to **Parc Nou** in **Olot** (**3h 40min**).

Walk 12: CAN SERRA • FAGEDA D'EN JORDÀ • VOLCÀ DE SANTA MARGARIDA • VOLCÀ DEL CROSCAT • CAN SERRA

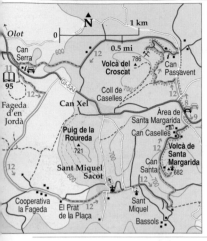

See also photo page 27

Distance: 10km/6.2mi; 2h45min

Grade: easy; 150m/490ft of ascent/descent along a well-signposted route (PNZVG Walks 1 and 15; see below). Suitable all year round, with the autumn colours in the beechwoods especially attractive, but avoid high summer.

Equipment: stout shoes, sunhat, cardigan, raingear, picnic, water

Access: 🚌 (Timetable 7c) or 🚗 to Can Serra (on the GI524, 3.4km southeast of Olot), or via Short walk 11

A part from the extensive lowland beechwood of the Fageda d'en Jordà (visited in Walk 11), the other highlight of the Parc Natural de la Zona Volcànica de La Garrotxa (PNZVG) is — as its name suggests — its spectacular volcanic landscape. Despite documented seismic activity over several centuries, the most recent eruption was that of Croscat — one of the focal points of this walk — which last blew its top some 11,500 years ago.

The walk starts at the **Can Serra** CAR PARK and INFORMATION CENTRE, open daily from 10.00-14.00 and 17.00-18.00 in summer or 15.00-16.00 in winter; closed midweek from mid-December to the end of February. (If you have opted to begin at Parc Nou in Olot and follow Short walk 11, you will reach Can Serra in 1h05min.)

From the information centre cross under the road and follow the path past the 'RESERVA NATURAL' sign and down steps between wooden hand-rails into the **Fageda d'en Jordà**. At the first signpost in the forest, with directions for the red-marked SENDER 1 to 'VOLCÀ DE STA. MARGARIDA' (also marked with RED DIAMONDS ON WOODEN POSTS), turn left to pass behind a

number of houses and then go right at the next sign. The path winds clearly through the somewhat featureless woodland and is always well-signposted at junctions, with small piles of rocks blocking false turns. In autumn, however, dead leaves may obscure the route, so *do* follow these directions. After three minutes a sign indicates that you should turn right, followed by a left turn two minutes later. Two minutes further on, turn right again, then left after one minute. Just under five minutes later, a vague path enters from the right; continue left here to reach a narrow road two minutes later (**15min**).

Turn right along this road, following the tarmac and ignoring tracks leading off on either side, to

Forest path in the Fageda d'en Jordà

arrive at a fork just under 10 minutes later, at the gates of the **Cooperativa La Fageda**. Bear left here on a narrow road passing the factory, then a plant NURSERY and a series of SETTLING POOLS on your right. At the gates of a well-appointed house (**Prat de la Plaça; 35min**), turn left along a track; then go right uphill immediately on a path which follows the edge of the forest. At a RED DIAMOND marker you begin to climb through the woods along a narrow, eroded path. In about five minutes the path tries to skirt round an area of bare rock, but it is best to walk up and over this rock for the last part of the climb. You reach a small SADDLE and an area of pastures dominated by a semi-ruined FARM (**50min**).
At this point — an excellent picnic spot — you pick up the tarmac of a minor road. Follow it downhill for 50m/yds, to the stately church of **Sant Miquel Sacot,** where you leave the road as it bears left and continue straight ahead down a track, with the church on your left. After 100m/yds, a RED DIAMOND marker points you to the right, down a rocky path. This shortly brings you to a track; turn right here and reach a small road where you should turn right once again (**55min**).
The volcano of Santa Margarida now lies straight ahead. After barely a minute's walking along the road, keep straight ahead at a crossroads along the GR-2, on the left-hand of two paths which head into the woods. On reaching a second crossroads, keep straight ahead, now along a track which ascends past exposed banks of volcanic lapilli on your left. After about 500m/yds, ignore a track heading down to the right just before reaching a junction, where you follow a small section of trail

up to the left, as signposted, to a SADDLE. Here a sign — indicating that you are now entering a *reserva natural* — points you up to the left. Wind up (ignoring a track off to the right at the second hairpin bend to the left) to the lip of the CRATER of **Santa Margarida**. Follow the path left along the lip of the crater and, at the first junction, turn right at a RED DIAMOND marker, down to a turreted house (**Can Santa**) built out of volcanic rock. At the gates of the house, turn right again along a track leading to the FLOOR OF THE CRATER, occupied by the attractive chapel of **Santa Margarida** (**1h20min**).
Retrace your steps to **Can Santa** and continue northeast along the lip of the crater, to signs to 'APARCAMENT' and 'VOLCÀ DEL CROSCAT'. After a minute, bear left, steeply downhill, along a track into the beechwoods. Then, once out of the forest, pass between a number of gargantuan twisted chestnuts, through which there are fine views northwards to the high Pyrenees. Drop down immediately

Views back to Sant Miquel Sacot on the way to the Volcà de Santa Margarida

through **Can Caselles**, bearing right out of the farmyard to descend to a crossroads, where you should turn left to the **Àrea de Santa Margarida** (1h40min) — a large CAR PARK on the Olot–Santa Pau road.

For the shorter, second part of the walk, follow the road to the left (northwest) for 200m/yds, then turn right along the broad entrance road towards **Càmping Lava**, now following signs marked 'SENDER 15: GREDERES DEL VOLCÀ CROSCAT'. Continue on the broad road between two restaurants — Santa Margarida and Les Forques — and then pass RESTAURANT MASNOU on your right. Here, you are indicated left up a track, signposted to the *grederes* (the abandoned quarries from which volcanic ash deposits were extracted for many years). The track peters out into a path, then bends right, into the forest. Just under 10 minutes later you reach the small interpretation centre at **Can Passavent** (2h), open 11.00-14.00 (all year) and 15.00-17.00 (winter) or 16.00-19.00 (summer). From here it is just a two-minute walk to the **Grederes** themselves, where a 10-minute circular route (illustrated

100

on page 27) reveals the surprisingly varied innards of the dormant volcano of **Croscat**, the largest in the Iberian Peninsula. Retrace your steps to Can Passavent (2h10min) and head east down a gently descending track which passes a small, colourful cliff on the right and rejoins the road from the three restaurants. *Note* signs reading 'Perill, esfondraments' (Danger, landslips) — in reference to the extremely friable nature of the rock here. Turn left, now signposted 'SENDER 1: FAGEDA D'EN JORDÀ', and then go left again as indicated, along an unsurfaced road which skirts the base of a small, rapidly eroding volcanic cliff on your left. At the gates to two houses (2h25min), keep left along the track, with a STONE WALL on your right. About five minutes later, turn right along a path which heads into the woods. Some 10 minutes of ups and downs bring you to a crossroads with a RED DIAMOND marker: turn left here, then go right alongside a house with a GREEN FENCE, to emerge at the CAR PARK at **Can Serra** (2h45min).

Walk 13: LA BISBAL • RIERA DE PASTELLS • SANT CEBRIÀ DE LLEDÓ • PUIG DE SANT MIQUEL • RIERA DE CANTAGALLS • MOLÍ D'EN FRIGOLA • LA BISBAL

Distance: 24km/15mi; 6h10min
Grade: moderate; a very long but relatively gentle walk, with just a couple of sharp ascents (totalling 300m/985ft). For the most part the route follows two PRs marked with yellow and white stripes. Despite abundant shade, high temperatures make this walk uncomfortable in midsummer, while heavy rains will swell the streams that you must ford en route. *Note: wild boar hunting is very popular here (see pages 54-55).*
Equipment: boots or stout shoes, sunhat, cardigan, raingear, picnic, water
Access: 🚗 (Car tour 4 at the 30.5km-point) or 🚌 (Timetables 8, 9) to La Bisbal
Short walk: River Daró — Riera de Pastells — Riera de Cantagalls — Molí d'en Frigola — River Daró. 11km/6.8mi;

2h50min. Season and equipment as for the main walk. Access by 🚗: drive to the village of Cruïlles (Car tour 4 at the 26km-point) and then use the map overleaf to head south to the **river Daró**, which you cross to park at the 45min-point in the main walk. Follow the main walk to the 2h20min-point (1h35min) then, instead of taking the first track back left towards Sant Cebrià, take the *second* track to the left heading northwest along the PR C1-00 (signposted 'CRUÏLLES'). After 15 minutes' placid walking through fairly open woodland, ignoring all turn-offs, this track winds steeply downhill into thicker forest and rejoins the main walk at the 4h25min-point (1h50min). From here follow the main walk back to the 5h25min-point, the **river Daró** (2h50min).

The thick cork and holm oak forests of Les Gavarres — a range of granite hills which peaks at 535m/1755ft (Puig d'Arques), barely 10km from the Mediterranean — provide a delightful contrast to the hubbub of the nearby coastal resorts. This walk takes you along some of the centuries-old paths which still link the agricultural plain of the Baix Empordà with ancient settlements such as that of Sant Cebrià de Lledó, secreted deep within the thick evergreen forests of

Pasture in Les Gavarres

the Gavarres, liberally sprinkled with tree heath and strawberry-tree. At Sant Cebrià, walkers can dine at Els Metges, a typical Catalan restaurant (closed Tuesdays and Wednesdays and the last fortnight in June and the first in July; (972 196102), which boasts gastronomy more typical of the mountains than the nearby Mediterranean.

Start the walk at the main road bridge over the often-dry **river Daró** in the centre of **La Bisbal**. One block east of the river, turn south along an unnamed street which immediately narrows and veers slightly to the right to become CARRER CAVALLERS. Continue along this street through the outskirts of the town until you can turn right down CARRER DE LA FONT DE L'ARBRE, signposted to the 'PISCINA MUNICIPAL' and 'FONT DE L'ARBRE'. Then, when the tarmac ends, keep straight on, with the **Daró** on your right *(note here the first yellow and white paint marks of the PR)*. Almost immediately, keep right at a Y-junction and cross a tributary of the Daró; then, after some 10 minutes' walking

between open fields and the Daró, enter a stand of umbrella pines which provides good shade for a picnic.

This whole area is a haven for wildlife, with cattle egret, bee-eater, hoopoe, crested lark, nightingale, melodious and fan-tailed warblers, golden oriole, serin and cirl bunting all common, and flowery waysides dominated in summer by sweet-smelling Spanish broom and the purple-flowered chaste tree with its five-fingered leaves, plus two composites: the pale pink galactites and the wickedly spiny milk thistle. After about 15 minutes of shade, turn right at a T-junction down to the Daró. Immediately after crossing another tributary on a footbridge, turn left

up an unsurfaced road next to a wooden sign indicating the PR-CI/03 (**45min**). *(This is where you park for the Short walk, and the main walk returns to this point.)* Pass between a number of large brick SHEDS and begin to ascend into the cork oaks. Turn left at the first crossroads and follow a sandy track downhill through fields, to meet the **Riera de Pastells** for the first time (**1h05min**). Follow the bed of the stream briefly to the right, then pick up a track heading up to the right. This bends left into the woods. Turn left at the next junction (all turns are indicated by the PR waymarks). Just as you approach the *riera*

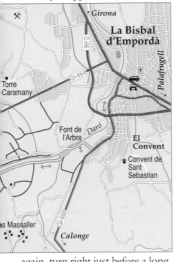

again, turn right just before a long, narrow field (*without* crossing the stream), along a shady path-cum-trail. Ignore a left turn after 50m/yds and continue on to the **Pont de les Dobles**. This bridge crosses the abandoned channel of one of the many watermills which operated in the Gavarres when the streams flowed much faster, at a time when these hills were populated by local people earning a living from the production of charcoal, glass, lime and even ice,

as well as from the harvesting of cork, pine kernels, honey and wild mushrooms (notably morels, Caesar's mushroom, saffron milk cap and chanterelle). Once across the bridge and over a short stretch of paved track, ford the alder- and ash-lined *riera* and follow the PR signs to the right along a deliciously shady, semi-sunken path hugging the *riera* to your right, to a junction with a narrow track (**1h20min**).

Turn left here, then cross the *riera* once more and travel through shady forest with straw foxglove and martagon lily along the wayside. Ignore the subsequent left and right turns before returning to the *riera* (**1h35min**). *Do not cross* here; instead turn right along a narrow path which follows the stream (on your left), then ford the *riera* about five minutes later, to come immediately to **Font de Can Marcader** on your left: a poor spring with distinctly iron-flavoured waters. Continue now with the stream on your right, until you join a broad track. This immediately drops down to the Riera de Pastells. Ignore the path and track off left, and cross the *riera* (**1h50min**), abandoning the PR-CI/03 and heading up and decidedly away from the stream on a broad track towards Can Font de Muntanya.

About 10 minutes later, look out for a fruit-laden (in June) wild cherry on your left. Then, after a major track joins from the left, you reach a multiple junction just beyond **Can Font** (**2h20min**). Turn back left here along the PR-CI/00, signposted to '*SANT CEBRIÀ DE LLEDÓ (ELS METGES)*'. *(But for the Short walk take the* second *left, along the PR-CI/00 towards Cruïlles.)*

Following yellow and white paint marks, drop down to a gully, where you ignore a track up to

Chaste tree (Vitex agnus-castus)

right and follow the bed of the gully south for 20m/yds, before continuing uphill to the right. On meeting a broad unsurfaced road (**2h40min**), turn left towards 'SANT CEBRIÀ', climbing all the while, to a well-deserved lunch or picnic at the ELS METGES bar/restaurant at **Sant Cebrià** (**3h10min**).

Once refreshed, take the steps leading down between the restaurant and the CHURCH, then turn right along an unsurfaced road. Pass an uninhabited FARM on your right, then wind down into and out of a gully. Ignore all the rather less-transited turn-offs, as well as two major left turns some 20 minutes and then a further 10 minutes beyond Sant Cebrià (**3h40min**). Five minutes after this second junction, two adjacent tracks head off to the right at different angles; take the second, uphill option, then immediately turn left to ascend the rocky outcrop known as **Puig de Sant Miquel** (220m/720ft). Continue along the track to the left of this modest peak, curving round beneath the summit. Then descend steeply to reach a cross-track, where you turn right, immediately passing through a METAL BARRIER. From here continue downhill to the uninhabited but far-from-abandoned farm of **Can Torrent** (**4h**). At the farm gates, turn back sharp left along a grassy track which contours around the top of a gully, then begins to descend gently. Meeting another track ascending from the *riera* below, keep straight on, soon ignoring a steep track up to the left. You gradually descend into the *riera*

three minutes later. Cross the stream three times in quick succession, to come to a stand of tall umbrella pines (**4h25min**). *(The PR-C1/00 and the Short walk enter from the right here.)* Continue straight ahead along a wide track lined with ragged-robin, large self-heal and the birthwort *Aristolochia longa* in early summer, listening out for Bonelli's warbler, firecrest, crested tit and short-toed tree-creeper in the forest.

Cross the *riera* again; around the next bend you will find a sign indicating the nearby **Font de Cantagalls** on your right. The main charm of this reliable if rather paltry spring, on the far side of what is now the **Riera de Cantagalls**, lies in its cool, shady setting beneath a truly enormous poplar and a canopy of alder, surrounded by sprays of soft shield-fern and clumps of martagon lilies and stinking iris. Back on the main track, you quickly cross the stream three times, before a long flat stretch, with the watercourse on your left, takes you out to the banks of the river **Daró** once more (**4h55min**). Ford the river and follow the plethora of signs which point you towards Cruïlles, passing behind a restored 17th-century watermill, the **Molí d'en Frigola**. The path behind the mill (still following the PR) brings you out at a PIG FARM, where you turn left along an unsurfaced road (**5h05min**) towards a group of rather desirable rustic homes.

From here the now-surfaced road heads straight towards Cruïlles, but you should turn right at the first crossroads, to head through open fields to **Can Girbau**. Then turn right again, back to the Daró and the point first encountered 45min into the walk (**5h25min**; *the Short walk ends here*). Now retrace your steps along the Daró to **La Bisbal** (**6h10min**).

Walk 14: PALAFRUGELL • TAMARIU • CALA PEDROSA • FAR DE SANT SEBASTIÀ • PALAFRUGELL

Distance: 14km/8.7mi; 3h55min
Grade: easy, but with a slightly tricky descent to Cala Pedrosa; the total altitude difference is just 170m/560ft. Good all year round except mid-summer.
Equipment: stout shoes, swim-wear, sunhat, cardigan, raingear, picnic, water
Access: 🚌 to Palafrugell (the 124km-point in Car tour 4) or 🚐 (Timetables 8, 10)
Short walk: Cala Pedrosa. 5km/ 3mi; 1h45min. Grade, equipment and season as above. Access by 🚌: take the GIV6591 (which later becomes the GIV6542) from Palafrugell towards Tamariu and park approximately 2.5km/ 1.5mi from the Palafrugell ring-road just before or just after the TURN-OFF TO FAR DE SANT SEBASTIÀ (the

The clear turquoise waters of Cala Pedrosa

50min-point in the main walk). Follow the main walk from here through **Tamariu** and **Cala Pedrosa**, but at the 2h25min-point turn *right,* back to the Palafrugell/Tamariu road. Follow this to the left for 10 minutes, to the TURN-OFF TO FAR DE SANT SEBASTIÀ.

This walk takes you through the typical coastal mosaic of fields and woods between Palafrugell and the small seaside resort of Tamariu, from there heading south along a rocky shore reminiscent of the pre-tourist Costa Brava. The route follows a combination of the green- and white-marked *sender local* (SL) linking Palafrugell and the lighthouse *(far)* of Sant Sebastià (the most powerful in Catalonia), the yellow-and white-marked PR-C/107 from Llafranc to Tamariu, and the red- and white-marked GR-92 coastal path.

Start the walk on the eastern outskirts of **Palafrugell**, next to the blue 'Comissaria' building of the Mossos d'Esquadra (the Catalan police force). Follow a green sign marked 'SENDER LOCAL — SANT SEBASTIÀ 1H9M' pointing you along CARRER DE RAMIR DEULOFEU. Almost immediately pick up an unsurfaced road on your right running parallel to the road. Just after passing a large solitary cork oak with the first GREEN AND WHITE WAYMARKS, bear right along CARRER DELS PLANS. After this road bears left, ignore a turn to the right; instead, continue alongside a STONE WALL, then keep

straight on at subsequent left and right turn-offs, passing a solitary, double-trunked cork oak to the left of the track (**15min**).
From here, the walk continues through fields, past a FARM on the right opposite another huge cork oak, then past a second FARM on the left. When you arrive at a multiple junction with floodlit TENNIS COURTS to your left, bear left, reaching a road in about five minutes (**25min**). Follow this road to the left, continuing until a sign, 'SANT SEBASTIÀ 41MIN', points you down a track to the right. Almost immediately, at a fork, take the right-hand option

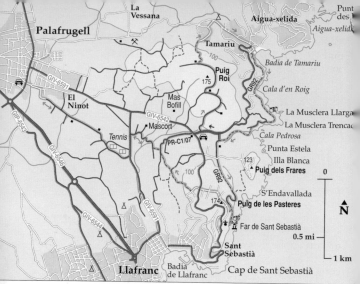

and continue between the tall FENCES AND HEDGES bordering a series of opulent second homes. Ignore a left turn between a row of cypress trees, then drop down into and climb out of a gully. Just where the track (normally closed off by a chain) veers right, bear left on a narrow, slightly overgrown but well-used path. This follows the edge of a field, to a broad track and a sign indicating your onward route left to 'TAMARIU', now along the yellow and white marked PR-C1/07 (40min).

On reaching a white house at a road junction (50min), follow the road signposted to 'TAMARIU', *not* towards 'Far de Sant Sebastià'. *(The Short walk begins and ends here.)* Soon, turn left down a track signposted 'TAMARIU', pass GREEN GATES on your left and start a gentle climb up a sunken track, into a pine forest. At the top of a rise after about 10 minutes, bear left at another GREEN GATE (on your right), with tantalising glimpses of the sea straight ahead. Keep left at a red and white HYDRANT by two houses (one white, one orange) on your right. At the next HYDRANT, turn right, soon swinging left to pass in front

of two more houses. Shortly, just before the next house (1h15min), leave the track by walking over a CHAIN on your right. Then turn left downhill immediately, following yellow and white waymarks on a narrow path into pines. After 10 minutes keep left at a T-JUNCTION of paths as the first houses come into view. Continue down into a gully, then up to the end of an asphalted road. Follow this down through a series of artlessly conceived second homes. Just after passing a couple of squat ugly apartment blocks ('Pins Mar') on your right, at a single metal railing, descend to the road again via a series of wooden steps (165 in all). Turn right to the beach at Tamariu (1h30min).

After a quick dip and/or picnic, head up the 11 steps to the south of the beach following the red and white GR-92 WAYMARKS and turn left immediately at a sign for 'CALA PEDROSA 35MIN' and 'SANT SEBASTIÀ 1H15MIN'. You then drop down immediately to a COVE, subsequently picking up the red and white waymarks again on the far side. The path from here on squeezes between walled gardens and the rocky coastal platform, through tall bushes of tree medick and tree mallow interspersed with exotic colonists such as prickly pear and Hottentot fig. After five minutes the path descends onto **Cala d'en Roig,** a bare expanse of rock housing a restored fisherman's hut and an interesting community of rock samphire and the sea-lavender *Limonium virgatum* (**1h45min**).

Follow the red and white marks across to the far side of this rocky cove, where the path continues up and over a fallen pine and heads towards a white house on the other side of a deep inlet. Pass below the house, turn right up a flight of steps, and then left into the pines, ignoring the start of a second set of steps. Following the red and white paint marks through the pines, you round the headlands of **La Musclera Llarga** and **La Musclera Trencada**. When the path meets a track, veer left, away from a white house up on your right, then ascend half-left alongside a row of planted cypresses, to where the track suddenly narrows to a path. Continue slightly uphill, climb to a wooden fence and then, next to a stone seat, zigzag down a steep, narrow path protected by a wooden fence, to pebbly **Cala Pedrosa** (**2h10min**).

Your onward path passes between two restored fishermen's HUTS and enters a surprisingly verdant gully. After two S-bends separated by a straighter stretch of path, you emerge on a broad track with fields beyond (**2h25min**), where you should turn left. (*But turn right for the Short walk.*) Still on the GR (as indicated by a sign, 'SANT SEBASTIÀ 30MIN'), you pass a house next to a carob grove on your left, then keep straight on at a crossroads. Continue gently uphill on a track — which soon becomes a path between FENCES — and into more pine woodland (**2h30min**).

This is the best-preserved forest habitat of the walk, housing splendid mature individuals of tree heath and strawberry-tree, banks of wonderfully fragrant, yellow-flowered shrubby scorpion-vetch and an abundance of the low-growing, crimson-flowered *Cistus crispus*. Shortly you veer up to the right at a fallen pine: soon bear left and then keep straight on to reach a series of steps that take you steeply up to a sign indicating 'PALAFRUGELL 58MIN' (straight on) or 'SANT SEBASTIÀ 4MIN' (to the left). Make the detour left to **Sant Sebastià** for spectacular views of the cliffs below the 15th-century WATCH-TOWER AND CHAPEL, before returning to the sign (**2h55min**) and continuing on towards Palafrugell.

Follow the GREEN AND WHITE WAYMARKS downhill past a big red and white 'X' on a tree (indicating that this is *not* the route for the coastal GR-92). On meeting a road, follow it downhill to the right, ignoring a road off left and keeping a STONE WALL on your right. Shortly, swing left down CARRER DE L'ARGENTINA. Just one minute later, turn left downhill again along CARRER DE CUBA. Go straight over a crossroads and then straight across another road and down CARRER DE FILIPINES. Before long, turn sharp right on a path opposite a yellow house. This takes you through scrubby mixed cork oak and pine woodland and emerges in a field. At this point, turn right and then immediately left, along a path heading towards the distant white houses of Palafrugell. Three minutes later you reach a track, where you turn right; after just 40m/yds you will find yourself back at the 'TAMARIU' sign you met at the 40min-point of the outward walk (**3h15min**). Turn left here and retrace your steps to **Palafrugell** (**3h55min**).

Walk 15: TORROELLA DE MONTGRÍ • CASA DE LES DUNES • MONTPLÀ • CASTELL DE MONTGRÍ • COLL DE LA CREU • TORROELLA DE MONTGRÍ

Distance: 8km/5mi; 2h50min
Grade: quite easy, with an initial ascent of 277m/910ft, followed by a descent/ascent of 100m/330ft and a final descent of 260m/855ft. The climb to the Castell de Montgrí is very steep. The walk (at its best in spring for the limestone flora) mostly follows the GR-92 and a *sender local*. In summer it is very hot; much of the north face of Montgrí around Santa Caterina was burnt in summer 2004.
Equipment: stout shoes, sunhat, cardigan, raingear, long trousers (prickly garrigue!), picnic, water
Access: 🚐 to Torroella de Montgrí (the 51km-point of Car tour 4) or 🚌 (Timetables 11, 12)
Short walks: both avoid the steep climb up to the Castell de Montgrí and are easy; access, equipment and season as above.

1 Torroella — Casa de les Dunes — Ermita de Santa Caterina — Coll de la Creu — Torroella. 6.5km/4mi; 2h05min. Follow the main walk as far as the SADDLE below Montplà (1h10min)

where, instead of turning left to ascend Montplà, you continue straight across the ridge and down to the chapel of **Santa Caterina.** Behind the chapel pick up the pleasant path signposted 'COLL DE LA CREU' which passes through some welcome shade and, after a gentle ascent, turns into a paved trail leading up to the **Coll de la Creu** (1h30min). Here you rejoin the main walk at the 2h15min-point and follow it to the end.

2 Torroella — Casa de les Dunes — Montplà — Coll d'en Garrigàs — Coll de la Creu — Torroella. 7km/4.4mi; 2h30min. Follow the main walk to the **Coll d'en Garrigàs** (1h40min), then descend a somewhat scree-strewn path to the right. This takes you to the halfway point on the path between Santa Caterina and the Coll de la Creu; turn left here to reach the **Coll de la Creu** (1h55min). Now follow the main walk from the 2h15min-point back to **Torroella.**

The karstified limestone of the Massís de Montgrí — in particular the rounded, castle-topped Muntanya de Santa Caterina — dominates the whole of the Baix Empordà plain. Together with the neighbouring flat-topped peak of Montplà, which is much less visited, it is renowned for spring-flowering bulbs, including almost 20 species of orchid. The pines planted in the 19th century to fix the continental dunes on the lower slopes of the massif boast surprisingly diverse butterfly communities, notably Moroccan orange tip and southern small white in early spring, marsh fritillary, southern white admiral and false ilex hairstreak in May, and tree and striped graylings and southern and Spanish gatekeepers in summer.

Start the walk at the CAMP DE FUTBOL *(zona esportiva)* in the northeast of **Torroella de Montgrí**. Take the unsurfaced road to the left of the football stadium; it immediately heads out into a mature olive grove. Ignore all turn-offs until you come to a more important junction (**10min**): turn left here, shortly passing a house with a PANTILED ROOF and GREEN GATES on your left. From here follow the track straight on (again ignoring all turn-offs), climbing gently through a fascinating mosaic of olive groves, orchards, vineyards, pine woodland and

flower-rich fallow, looking out for birds such pallid and alpine swifts, crag martin, blue rock thrush, black redstart, Sardinian warbler, raven and serin.

The garrigue here is a glorious assemblage of holly oak, lentisc, grey-leaved cistus, rosemary, the winter-flowering heather *Erica multiflora*, Spanish broom and the sweet-smelling lavender *Lavandula latifolia*, all entwined with fragrant clematis, the typical Mediterranean honeysuckle *Lonicera implexa*, wild madder and common smilax. Eventually you arrive at the **Casa de les Dunes** (**45min**) on the left, a summer camp for children. It makes an ideal picnic spot.

Turn left just beyond this house, to a multi-lingual INFORMATION PANEL explaining the origin of the continental dunes on which you are now standing. Continue past the panel, heading straight on along an unsurfaced road. (Ignore the GR-92 off to the left sign-posted 'Castell de Montgrí'; it's a short but rather treacherous scramble up a scree slope to Montplà.) Soon, where the road swings right, continue straight ahead along a track through light pine woodland (good for giant

Grey-leaved cistus (Cistus albidus), *with Montplà and the Illes Medes in the background*

From the summit head west along the GR, after a couple of minutes ignoring a path off to the left and then keeping left along the GR at a junction. Now you descend in earnest to the **Coll d'en Garrigàs** (**1h40min**), the saddle between Montplà and Montgrí. *(Short walk 2 drops down to the right here.)* Carry on straight ahead, starting to climb so steeply that you may have to use your hands in places. *(The GR waymarks are rather indistinct and widely spaced here.)* Having struggled up to the **Castell de Montgrí** atop the **Muntanya de Santa Caterina** (**1h55min**), you will find it always open and with an interesting information panel inside.

In front of the castle entrance, the GR continues west and then zig-zags down to the **Coll de la Creu** (**2h15min**), where it meets a path on the right coming up from the chapel of Santa Caterina. *(Both Short walks rejoin the main walk here.)* At this point, turn left down a rocky path (still the GR), past two empty CHAPELS. On reaching a third CHAPEL, be sure to pick up the lower path (*not* the GR), which descends gradually through the pines. You rejoin the GR in five minutes, for a final downhill stretch between pomegranate trees bursting with fruit in autumn. Reaching the outskirts of **Torroella** opposite a white building, turn left uphill along a narrow road. Shortly, turn right along RONDA PAU CASALS, an un-surfaced road in front of another white building. Pass a school and return to the CAMP DE FUTBOL (**2h50min**).

orchids in March), which becomes a path as you pass a field and RUINED FARM on your right. The path begins to climb and, just after a steeper, gouged-out section, another path enters from the right. Keep left here to begin the final ten-minute climb up to a SADDLE on the ridge (**1h10min**).

Turn left along the ridge, bright with the purple or yellow flowers of *Iris lutescens* in March. *(But for Short walk 1, go straight over the saddle and down to Santa Caterina.)* After passing over a small rise, you drop down to another small SADDLE. From here the path rises again towards a white fire-watch hut. In the meantime the GR-92 enters from your left (keen botanists should detour briefly along this route to investigate the cliffs for clumps of tufted catchfly and an isolated colony of the bushy, prickly crucifer *Hormatho-phylla spinosa*). Continue to climb steeply up the southerly continuation of the GR, passing within 30m/yds of the FIRE-WATCH HUT, to reach the Montplà plateau. Keep along the GR — straight towards the Castell de Montgrí in the southwest. You wind through prickly garrigue *above* the south-facing cliffs, to where a red- and yellow-striped Catalan flag flutters at the SUMMIT of **Montplà** (317m/1040ft; **1h30min**).

Walk 16: L'ESTARTIT • CALA PEDROSA • CALA FERRIOL • TORRE PONÇA • L'ESTARTIT

See also photograph of nearby Cap de la Barra on page 34
Distance/time: 8km/5mi; 2h50min
Grade: easy-moderate, with an initial ascent of 130m/425ft, but then two descents/ascents of 140m/460ft down to sea level and back, which are quite steep in places, with loose stones underfoot. The walk mostly follows a *sender local* and the GR-92. Undoubtedly best in the spring, when the limestone flora is at its peak; very hot in summer.
Equipment: stout shoes, sunhat, swimwear, cardigan, raingear, picnic, water
Access: 🚗 to L'Estartit (the 57km-point on Car tour 4) or 🚌 (Timetables 12, 12a)
Short walk: L'Estartit — Torre Ponça — L'Estartit. 4km/2.5mi; 1h05min. Easy; access as main walk. This walk follows surfaced minor roads; light footwear will suffice. Follow the main walk to the T-junction at the 25min-point, then turn left along the road to rejoin the main walk at the 2h10min-point (35min), dropping back down via **Torre Ponça** into **L'Estartit** (**1h15min**).

The limestone massif of Montgrí presents an abrupt face to the sea, far too irregular and inaccessible for even the most determined of speculators to have defiled its beauty. This walk takes you across the garrigue-covered plateau before dropping down to two remote and idyllic coves — perfect for spring picnics and a dip in the Mediterranean. March sees an explosion of colourful bulbs — rush-leaved jonquil, dull ophrys, giant orchid, sand crocus and both yellow and purple forms of *Iris lutescens* — while the whole area is painted pink and white when the cistuses bloom en masse in April.

Start the walk from the CHURCH in the PLAÇA DE L'ESGLÉSIA in **L'Estartit**: turn inland along the PEDESTRIAN PRECINCT, almost immediately taking the first right along CARRER DEL PONT NOU and then the first left. Here a sign indicating a *sender local* points you right up PUJADA DE LA PRIMAVERA towards 'CALA PEDROSA 1HR' and 'CALA FERRIOL 1HR 32MIN'. Head steeply up the tarmac past the green gates of CÀMPING L'ESTARTIT, ignoring a path off to the left signposted to Torre Moratxa and Roca Maura. About 100m/yds further on, follow the road to the right towards 'L'ESCALA' (**15min**). *(Both the main and Short walks return to this point.)* As this road flattens out, clumps of *Iris lutescens*

111

Iris lutescens

thrive amid the scrub in spring, while there are excellent views west to the Castell de Montgrí (Walk 15) and northwest to the impressive mansion known as Torre Ponça.

At a T-junction of roads (**25min**) head straight across (slightly to your left), to pick up a stony track with a *sender local* SIGNPOST. *(But for the Shorter walk, turn left on the road.)* Soon you enter a low pine forest and, as the trees thin out and you enter an area of low garrigue — dominated by holly oak, rosemary and, above all, grey-leaved cistus, you are rewarded by fine views north to Cap de Creus (Walk 20). About five minutes later, turn left at a crossroads of tracks (GREEN AND WHITE WAY-MARKS, but *no* signpost) and start dropping down through the pines towards Cala Pedrosa. Before long you reach the floor of a shady gully, which you then follow all the way down to the sea at **Cala Pedrosa** (**50min**). The coastal rocks here are adorned with clumps of silver ragwort, rock samphire and the sea lavender *Limonium minutum.*

Your onward route is indicated by green and white waymarks about 30m/yds from the water's edge on the north side of the cove. BLUE ARROWS also show the way up a rather indistinct but well-waymarked path through the pines and out onto the edge of the cliff above — a spectacular picnic spot, with stunning views north to La Roca Foradada (a sea-cliff pierced with a hole at sea level, traversed by the tourist boats from L'Estartit). Continue following the green and white waymarks along a narrow, rocky path, rising through the garrigue, until you come to a junction of paths (**1h10min**). Turn right towards 'CALA FERRIOL', first descending gently and then dropping down more steeply to reach the water's edge at **Cala Ferriol** (**1h30min**). From this cove retrace your steps back up to the junction first encountered at the 1h10min-point (**1h50min**), then turn right. Continue west towards the next signpost, just visible on the horizon ahead. On reaching the SIGN, turn left along the GR-92, reaching presently an open area where the path drops down slightly to the left between stunted olives. Note here another signpost, where the GR-92 turns right.*

Continue straight ahead downhill towards L'Estartit, almost immediately reaching the metalled road you crossed at the 25min-point (**2h10min**; *the Shorter walk rejoins the main walk here*).

Turn right here and then ignore a right turn to L'Escala immediately afterwards. Continue downhill along the tarmac to the gates of **Torre Ponça** (**2h25min**). This estate boasts a magnificent house — surely everybody's dream home! — and is a haven for wild-life, harbouring legions of small birds, giant orchids in the verges in spring and semi-wild boar in the fields.

Ten minutes further down the road you reach the junction you first encountered after 15min; from here continue straight on down the hill and back to **L'Estartit** (**2h50min**).

---

*The GR would take you to the Casa de Les Dunes above Torroella in 1h, where you could link up with Walk 15.

Walk 17: CASTELLÓ D'EMPÚRIES • ESTANY EUROPA • EL CORTALET • LA MASSONA • EL CORTALET • CASTELLÓ D'EMPÚRIES

Distance: 21km/13mi; 4h10min
Grade: easy, with no discernible altitude difference, although rather long (especially for hot weather). This route can also be muddy and sometimes subject to strong *tramuntana* winds. The walk partly follows the GR-92 and routes marked by the Aiguamolls de l'Empordà Natural Park. Good all year round for birds.
Equipment: waterproof shoes, sunhat, cardigan, picnic, water, insect repellent, binoculars
Access: 🚌 to Castelló d'Empúries (the 132km-point in Car tour 5) or 🚌 (Timetables 13, 14, 15)
Short walks
1 Castelló d'Empúries —
Estany Europa — El Cortalet — Castelló d'Empúries. 10km/6.2mi; 2h30min. Grade, equipment and access as for the main walk. Follow the main walk to **El Cortalet** (1h35min) and then head straight back along the GR-92 to **Castelló d'Empúries** without following the Massona trail.
2 El Cortalet — La Massona — El Cortalet. 7km/4.4mi; 1h40min. Easy; equipment as for the main walk; access by 🚌 to El Cortalet. Simply follow the trail to **La Massona** from El Cortalet information centre to the beach and back — a short and easy option for birdwatchers.

The low-lying hinterland of the Bahia de Roses was once a huge, malarial marshland, exploited only for hunting, fishing and cattle-rearing. Decades of drainage to produce land suitable for agriculture and hotel complexes have taken their toll, however, so that the only sizeable area of marsh remaining is the Aiguamolls de l'Empordà, saved by public outcry in the 1980s and protected as a *parc natural*. Today it is one of the most exciting birdwatching sites in Catalonia, harbouring a huge variety of species in a relatively small area, and well equipped with hides and observation towers. The labyrinth of lagoons, reed-beds and brackish pastures close to the sea which we will explore during this walk is particularly renowned for breeding purple herons, little bitterns, marsh harriers, black-winged stilts and purple gallinules, with all manner of waders, terns and warblers passing through on migration.

White storks' nest at Peralada (Car tour 5, beyond Castelló d'Empúries)

The Estanys del Matà: looking towards the observation point atop the highest silo (2h)

The walk starts outside the HOTEL EMPORIUM, on the old Figueres–Roses road, at the southern edge of the town of **Castelló d'Empúries**. Head northeast along the road for about 10 minutes, until you come to the excellent **Butterfly World** on your left (open from 10.00-20.00 in July and August, but closing earlier in spring and autumn; closed completely from November to March; ☎ 972 450761). Turn right here along the road towards Empuriabrava and, as you are about to pass under the Castelló d'Empúries BYPASS, take a track up the bank on your right. Pass through a wooden BARRIER and continue straight ahead along the contention DYKE for the left bank of the **river Muga**. About 20 minutes later, cross a WOODEN FOOTBRIDGE over the Muga, to reach the gates of the **Empuria-brava** WATER TREATMENT PLANT ('Depuradora' on the map; **40min**); here blue signs and POSTS WITH BLUE PAINT point you towards ESTANY EUROPA and EL CORTALET.

Walk along the track, with the water treatment plant on your left, then bear left after 200m/yds at a T-junction. You soon arrive at the 114

first of three HIDES *(aguaits)* on your left that overlook the **Estany Europa**. This artificial lagoon is often the only part of the reserve to hold water in high summer, and it's an excellent place to see greater flamingos and purple gallinules. From the hide continue along the track, turning right along the perimeter path of the lake and passing the **Aguait dels Capons**. Then take a path off right to the nearby **Aguait de les Miloques**. From this latter hide, return to the track and continue to the right towards 'EL CORTALET', soon reaching an unsurfaced road. Turn left to arrive at the entrance posts of **Can Comes**. Take the right-hand option to circumnavigate this farm, then continue for 1km/0.6mi, to reach a METAL FENCE and crossroads of tracks (**1h20min**).

Turn *left* here for a 20-minute return detour to the HIDE overlooking the **Estany d'en Túries** *(not included in walk timings)*, or turn right to continue on towards El Cortalet, passing a RUINED FARM on your right and then the **Aguait dels Roncaires** on your left, overlooking the extensive **Estany de Cortalet**.

Just as you are approaching **El**

Cortalet, follow a path through a WOODEN GATE to the left — to the **Aguait Quim Franch** (1h35min). Then walk on 50m/yds, to the excellent INFORMATION CENTRE AND SHOP (open from 09.30-14.00 and 15.30-18.00 in winter; from 10.30-15.00 and 16.30-19.00 in summer).

Turn right out of the doors to pick up the **Massona Trail** (coinciding here with the GR-92), which heads south towards the beach, passing a series of strategically placed hides en route. Initially you turn left (or *right for Short walk 1*) along a tree-lined track, kinking left and then right over a STREAM to pass several CAGES on the right, used in the successful reintroduction of the white stork to the area. A little further on, a short track heads left to the **Aguait de les Gantes**; then, on the right, a WOODEN WALKWAY climbs to the **Observatori de les Daines** viewing platform. Once back on the main track, you follow a broad ditch fringed with a gallery forest of white and black poplars, white willow, alder, narrow-leaved ash and many dead small-leaved elms, until you come to a T-junction (**1h55min**). Turn left here to the **Observatori Pallejà** — or go right over a WOODEN BRIDGE to reach the **Estanys del Matà**, an area of former rice paddies being restored to natural marsh vegetation by a herd of Camargue horses. This is now an excellent place to observe purple gallinules, black-winged stilts and passage waders. At the edge of these *estanys*, turn right for a short detour to an OBSERVATION POINT perched atop the highest of three white rice SILOS (**2h**; there are also toilets here).

Retrace your steps to the T-junction at the edge of the Estanys del Matà (**2h10min**), then follow signs towards 'LES LLAUNES', passing the **Aguait del Gall Marí** on your left. Continue along a section of raised BOARD-WALK. Pass signs to the **Aguait del Bruel** on the left, then turn left at the WOODEN GATES, to walk almost immediately over a SLUICE GATE/BRIDGE. From here, skirt the back of a campsite to reach the BEACH and an OBSERVATION TOWER (**2h30min**). *Note: during the Kentish plover breeding season (from April 1 to June 15) the beach to the north is closed to walkers, and the Massona trail ends here (but see the 'Option' at the end of the walk).*

Retrace your steps along the Massona trail to **El Cortalet** (**3h15min**). Instead of entering the building, continue straight on through the car park along the GR-92, until the access road bends sharp left. Turn right here along an unsurfaced road. In 30 minutes this takes you to **Mas Feliu**, on the road directly below the embankment of the Castelló d'Empúries BYPASS. Turn right here and, when the road bears right in just over 1km/0.6mi, turn left on a track that drops down to a FORD (usually with only a trickle of water) over the **river Muga**. Climb the bank on the far side of the river to meet the road from Castelló d'Empúries that you followed at the beginning of the walk; turn left here to return to **Castelló d'Empúries** (**4h10min**).

Option

Outside April 1-June 15, you can head north from the 2h30min-point. Walk along the beach for 40 minutes (2.3km/1.4mi), to a track cutting inland. Turn left here, to arrive 20 minutes later at the crossroads first encountered at the 1h20min-point. From here retrace your steps to Castelló d'Empúries. *Note: the beach is often flooded and impassable in autumn and winter, so be sure to check conditions at the information centre beforehand.*

Cork oaks near the Vilaüt lagoons (Walk 18)

Walk 18: LES TORROELLES • ESTANY DE VILAÜT • VILAÜT • LA TORRE DEL VENT • LES TORROELLES

See also photograph opposite
Distance: 7.5km/4.7mi; 1h45min
Grade: very easy, with an ascent/descent of just 35m/115ft. Mud and the sometimes-unrelenting strong north wind (the infamous *tramuntana*) are the only possible difficulties. The walk partly follows the GR-92. Interesting all year round, although very hot in summer
Equipment: waterproof footwear (failing that, three plastic bags — one for each foot and one to store the wet bags in your rucksack! — can get you through even the deepest puddles), wind-proof jacket, cardigan, sunhat, picnic, water, insect repellent, binoculars
Access: ▦ to Restaurant Aiguamolls in the hamlet of Les Torroelles (Car tour 5) — 2.5km/1.5mi southwest of Palau-saverdera on the GIV6103 to Castelló d'Empúries (a road not marked on Michelin maps).
Short walk: Restaurant

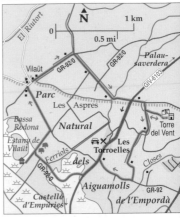

Aiguamolls — Vilaüt — Restaurant Aiguamolls.
5km/3.1mi; 1h10min. Same grade, equipment and access as for the main walk. Follow the main walk to the 1h-point, then turn right along the road to reach the Restaurant Aiguamolls ten minutes later.

T his walk explores the Vilaüt sector of the Aiguamolls Natural Park. Far less visited than the area centred on El Cortalet, it is characterised by a series of low, rounded granite outcrops around the freshwater Estany de Vilaüt. The whole area — known as Les Aspres ('the rough area') — is presided over to the north by the Muntanya de Verdera, topped by the Castell de Sant Salvador (670m/2200ft; see page 46), with the mountains of the Garrotxa and the peak of Canigó in French Catalonia visible in the distance.

The walk starts at the RESTAU-RANT AIGUAMOLLS in **Les Torroelles**, whose owners kindly allow visitors to the *parc natural* to use its car park. Turn south along the road, soon noting (by a STONE HUT) the red-and white GR WAY-MARKS entering from the left; *this is your return route at the end of the walk*. After about five minutes, turn right through a METAL GATE under a PYLON along the GR-92/0 towards 'PALAU-SAVERDERA'. You

now come into an area of curvilinear GRANITE OUTCROPS, some of which are still clothed with remnants of the region's former forests, dominated by downy and cork oaks. In spring the dry grasslands here harbour tassel hyacinths and diminutive conical orchids, while the damp ditches are home to tree lavatera — a favourite of gardeners — and the hedgerows are thick with Christ's-thorn, distinguished in

117

Christ's-thorn (Paliurus spina-christi)

summer by its papery, disc-shaped fruits.

Follow the track as it bends first to the left then to the right. In ten minutes you come to a junction of tracks marked by two mature CORK OAKS that provide good shade for a picnic (**20min**; photograph page 116). Turn left here for a five-minute return detour to a HIDE overlooking the **Estany de Vilaüt**, for good views of waders, duck and herons. Back at the cork oaks, continue northeast to a crossroads of tracks, where you should turn left through fields alive with flocks of lapwings, skylarks, crested larks, finches and corn buntings in winter, in summer attracting such sought-after birds as great-spotted cuckoo, roller and lesser grey shrike. Eventually you arrive at the three farms which constitute the small settlement of **Vilaüt**. Leave the first farm on your left (**35min**), then immediately turn right along an unsurfaced road, passing in front of the METAL GATES of the next farm. On entering the third farmyard (with dogs of the tail-wagging, non-barking ilk), carry on straight ahead along a track heading northeast, following a CONCRETE WATER CONDUIT (the first of many), initially on your right and then on your left.

Carry on past a RUINED FARM and vineyards on your left. At a crossroads of tracks (**45min**), turn right (southeast), leaving the GR and picking up another WATER CONDUIT. Follow this faithfully, past a GREEN HUT on your right

and through a copse of pines. You pass a group of farm buildings on your right, at which point the track bends left to cross a stream and continues until it reaches the GIV6103 road (**1h**). *(The Short walk turns right here.)*

Continue straight over the road onto a track, which passes a white-fenced STABLES on the left and then bears right after 200m/yds. Almost immediately, just before the track passes through another WATER CONDUIT, turn left along a track at the edge of a VINEYARD. At first this track is rather indistinct, but it becomes more defined and leads towards a low wooded summit. When the track fizzles out, pick up goat paths to reach a restored watchtower (**La Torre del Vent**; **1h15min**), perched amid a few cork oaks on the top of this unprepossessing hill. At just over 50m/165ft, this represents the high-point of the Empordà plain and is an excellent place for a picnic among hill-topping swallowtails and scarce swallowtails.

Returning to the main track five minutes later, turn left (south) through the WATER CONDUIT and then bear right at a scruffy SHACK along a track with another WATER CONDUIT on your left. Ignore a right turn almost immediately. Before long, pass through the conduit and then turn left as the conduit heads off to the right. Shortly, at a HUT, bear right and follow the track as far as a T-junction (**1h35min**), where you encounter the GR-92 once again. Turn right here, to reach the STONE HUT first passed near the start of the walk, then turn right along the road for the final 200m/yds back to the RESTAURANT AIGUAMOLLS in **Les Torroelles** (**1h45min**).

Distance: 11km/6.8mi; 3h30min
Grade: moderate; despite being relatively short, the succession of ups and downs on uneven paths makes this a surprisingly tiring walk, especially on a windy day. There are a few short sections along the edge of sheer (but very low) cliffs on the last section of the walk, where you must be sure-footed and have a head for heights. The limestone flora is at its best in early spring; avoid high summer, when it is very hot.
Equipment: stout shoes, sunhat, cardigan, long trousers, raingear, windproof clothing, picnic, water
Access: 🚌 (the 85km-point on Car tour 6); park at the Montjoi 'Ciutat de Vacances' campsite and holiday complex.

Short walk: Circuit of Cap de Norfeu. 9km/5.6mi; 2h40min. Easy, taking in the best of Cap de Norfeu's limestone habitats without having to negotiate the vertiginous cliff sections; access and equipment as above. From **Montjoi**, walk southeast along the unsurfaced coast road until you meet the 1h20min-point of the main walk at the 'neck' of **Cap de Norfeu** (**45min**). From here, follow the main walk as far as the 2h40min-point (**2h**), then return to the 'neck' by heading downhill to the right (northeast) on the GR-92 for five minutes. Retrace your steps to Montjoi along the unsurfaced coast road, arriving back at **Montjoi** (2h40min).

A lthough essentially part of the pronounced headland of Cap de Creus (see Walk 20), the southerly promontory of Cap de Norfeu is of interest in its own right, given that for the most part it comprises pale limestones and houses a rich and distinctive flora. Furthermore, the tip of Cap de Norfeu is one of the best sea-watching points in Catalonia, especially for Cory's shearwaters in spring (see also Walk 20).

The walk starts at the *CIUTAT DE VACANCES HOLIDAY COMPLEX* at **Montjoi**. Continue southeast along the unsurfaced coastal road, soon turning left up a track signposted *'CALA JÚNCOLS PER L'INTERIOR'*. *(But for the Short walk, continue along the unsurfaced road.)* Follow the track in a hairpin to the right but, when it hairpins to the left, continue straight on across the hillside on a narrow path, heading through the typical Cap de Creus scrub of sage-leaved and narrow-leaved cistuses, Mediterranean mezereon, *Ruta angustifolia*, French lavender, lentisc, rosemary and thorny broom. Soon the path crosses over a sheltered gully and starts to rise beside the *WALLS* of a long-abandoned vineyard. A *SADDLE* (**25min**) makes an ideal

picnic spot, with excellent views of Cap de Norfeu to the southeast. For those with extra energy, a short climb south will take you up Puig de la Morisca, for even better views of the coast (10 minutes return; *not* in the timings). The continuation of your route is the obvious path running north from the saddle, which climbs quite steeply and unevenly (*care: loose rocks!*) up to a WALL on your right. Turn right here, along a narrow path, to reach a broad track a couple of minutes later. Turn right again and head downhill for 25 minutes (through an area burnt in 2001), before once again encountering the unsurfaced coast road (**1h**). Cross straight over the road and follow a track towards an obvious

Tree spurge (Euphorbia dendroides) *and* Coronilla minima*; below: sea mallow* (Lavatera maritima) *and* Coronilla minima *on Cap de Norfeu*

ROCKY OUTCROP, from which there fine views down into **Cala Jóncols**. A rather indistinct path skirts the northern flank of the outcrop, but quickly fades out, obliging you to pick your way southeast down through abandoned terraces.

Meet the GR-92 at another small SADDLE and follow it to the right, dropping down into a surprisingly humid gully occupied by fragrant myrtle bushes, then climb to join the unsurfaced coastal road again at the 'NECK' of **Cap de Norfeu**

(**1h20min**). *(The Short walk joins here.)* At this point, head southeast along a broad track, now with red diamond waymarking. This eventually narrows to a path, bringing you to a CAVE, once a hermitage, with an explanatory panel in English. Note the white intrusion of marble all but passing through the cave, as well as a sign warning you not to stray from the footpaths in the Cap de Norfeu reserve. Continue southeast, ignoring a sign pointing right, up to the 'Cova les Encantades' just as the rock underfoot changes to limestone. Shortly you reach a group of large pines, immediately after which you ascend to the base of a CLIFF (**1h40min**).

Now on the limestone, grey-leaved cistus replaces the acid-loving sage-leaved and narrow-leaved cistuses and French lavender, with interesting plants to look out for including the honeysuckle *Lonicera implexa*, butcher's broom, delightful pale-green mounds of tree spurge down to your left, pink-flowered cushions of *Erodium crispum* on bare outcrops and, in March, clumps of the white-flowered, many-headed *Narcissus dubius*.

Before long, this delightful path climbs quickly up onto the Cap de Norfeu plateau, where the thin limestone soils are dotted with wind-sculpted clumps of *Coronilla minima* and, in autumn, carpeted with the delicate blooms of autumn narcissus and autumn squill. Head south (inland), to a signposted T-junction (**1h50min**), where you turn left for a ten-minute walk to the TIP OF **Cap de Norfeu**, where the cliffs are swathed in silver ragwort, tragacanth and sea mallow (**2h**). Just before the end of the cape and the remains of a stone hut, turn right at a wooden post and begin a circuit of the headland. In five

minutes you reach an INFORMATION BOARD ('La Punta de Norfeu'), from where the path curves to the right along the cliff-top. After the path begins to drop quite steeply and then climbs briefly, you reach a signposted T-junction.

Head left (northwest)* for 10 minutes to reach the **Torre de Norfeu** (**2h30min**), a 16th-century watchtower endowed with another information panel. From here continue along the path, turning right almost immediately down through a CLEFT in the cliffs. The steep, rocky path takes you to a junction of paths (**2h40min**). *(The Short walk continues straight on at this junction.)*

Turn left here and drop down towards the southwestern flank of the headland, now back on the GR-92. The steep path, with a series of large steps, descends half-right to a diminutive COVE and another information panel. From here follow the GR along the cliff-edge *(risk of vertigo)* and down to a BEACH, then continue alongside a wall lined with prickly pear to the **Platja del Calitjar** (**3h**). At the far end of this beach, climb the steps below the white house to reach the last section of roller-coaster cliff path. Eventually the GR signs point you back up to the unsurfaced coastal road. Turn left here for a 15-minutes stroll back to **Montjoi** (**3h30min**).

---

*Or turn right, to return to the T-junction at the 1h50min-point.

Walk 20: PORT DE LA SELVA • SANT BALDIRI • CALA TAVALLERA • PRAT DE ROMAGÓS • CAP DE CREUS • PORTLLIGAT • CADAQUÉS

Distance: 23km/14.3mi; 6h
Grade: moderate; the length and continual ups and downs make this a rather tiring walk. The route follows the GR-11 for much of the way, although the waymarking is poor or ambiguous in places.
Equipment: boots or stout shoes, sunhat, cardigan, compass, picnic, water
Access: 🚌 to Port de la Selva or Cadaqués (the 28- and 45km-points in Car tour 6) or 🚐 (Timetables 13-16); taxi to start or at the end of the walk. Few paths cross the rugged interior of Cap de Creus, and to show you

the *best* of the area, our walk relies on being able to get from back from Cadaqués to Port de la Selva at the end of the walk (or to start out) by pre-arranged taxi. This route is spectacular all year round, but avoid high summer or days when the *tramuntana* is blowing fiercely.
Short walk: Port de la Selva — Cala Tavallera — Port de la Selva. 10km/6.2mi; 3h40min. Easy-moderate; same equipment as the main walk; access by 🚌 or 🚐 to Port de la Selva. Follow the main walk to **Cala Tavallera** (**1h50min**); return the same way.

It is hard to believe that the bleak but visually stunning landscape of Cap de Creus was once so densely covered with evergreen oak forests that access to most of the peninsula was easier by sea than by land. Since that time, however, most of the peninsula has been cleared and profitably cultivated, although today this is also almost impossible to imagine, as the *Phylloxera* plague of 1879 virtually wiped out the vineyards in one fell swoop. Today the windswept slopes of the Cap de Creus are characterised above all by abandoned terraces, clothed with sweeping expanses of small-flowered gorse, thorny broom, narrow- and sage-leaved cistuses, tree heath and green heather.

The walk starts at the northern end of the peaceful harbour of **Port de la Selva**. Follow signs to 'ZONA PORTUARIA'. As you reach the last houses, you will see a sign to 'PLATJA TAMARIUA' as well as the first sign for the GR-11, indicating your route. Follow the road around the headland of **Punta de la Creu** to a crossroads, where you turn right up a road to 'SANT BALDIRI DE TAVALLERA' and 'CAP DE CREUS'. Walk steeply up past houses on your right, with fine views down into **Cala Tamariua** on your left. At another junction, next to an isolated white house, keep left. On reaching a third junction, where CARRER EMPORDÀ

heads down steeply to the right into Port de la Selva, continue straight ahead on an unsurfaced road with red waymarks (this is walk 6 of the Parc Natural del Cap de Creus and also signposted 'SANT BALDIRI DE TAVALLERA S.X.'; **20min**).
After about 1km/0.6mi, the unsurfaced road swings over a gully, where the extra moisture provides a foothold for the striking deep pink flowers of tree lavatera. A further 1km takes you to a sign indicating 'PUIGNAU' to the left — a ruined farm just visible through the pines. Keep an eye open here for hoopoe, turtle dove and melodious warbler. Keep straight

122

on here, shortly reaching a T-junction (**55min**) where you turn right towards 'MAS D'EN PALTRÉ' and 'CALA TAVALLERA'. After barely 100m/yds, take the *second* track on the left, bordered by a DRYSTONE WALL with a pine plantation on its right. Descend to a small building with an attached CAGE-LIKE STRUCTURE at a junction, then continue straight ahead downhill on a track signposted to 'SANT BALDIRI'. This becomes a path and soon drops down to meet another track. At this point go straight ahead again, descending past an open grassy area on the right, into an area of mature cork oaks. You soon arrive at the overgrown ruins of **Sant Baldiri de Tavallera** (**1h05min**), a small nucleus of houses huddled around a church and defence tower. Just beyond Sant Baldiri, a sign points you towards 'CALA TAVALLERA' and 'MAS D'EN PALTRÉ' along a narrow but distinct path which climbs up and out of the woods and then down into mature cork and downy oak forest surrounding a deliciously shady gully (**1h15min**). This is a good place to search for stripe-necked terrapins, viperine snakes and Iberian pool frogs. Cross the stream and head up steeply to the left on a path that passes the green chain-link fence of **Mas d'en Paltré** before coming to a broad track (**1h25min**). Turn left here and continue for just over 10 minutes, accompanied by marvellous views northwards. Just after a section between two STONE WALLS, you are indicated left along another track; this soon becomes a path, then rejoins the track you have just left. From here the stony descent to **Cala Tavallera** (**1h50min**) is obvious.
Your onward route out of the cove takes you east along the shingle beach, past the dry, stony bed of a stream which occasionally flows into the *cala*. Pick up a path climbing steeply up to the right (just before a wooden 'CAP DE CREUS' sign). The path ascends quickly past wind-pruned prickly junipers and sprawling mats of sage-leaved cistus and lentisc, with cushions of Pyrenean pink and clumps of *Polycarpon polycarpoides* decorating the cliffs. You reach the base of a weather-pitted cliff to your left. At this point a gentler gradient provides some respite, before a further steep section takes you up to and between THREE ISOLATED PINES. Swing left here and, on reaching the base of another very eroded cliff, bear right onto the start of another moderate uphill stretch, the end of which is marked by a *'Reserva Integral'* sign (**2h10min**). Now descending gently, you soon reach an expanse of GRASSLAND, with the white-washed, pantile-roofed farm of **Mas de la Birba** lying 400m/yds away to your right. Continue straight ahead here; then, after a short rocky uphill section, carry straight on across another grassy area, where you pick up a track coming from Mas de la Birba. Head straight on up the track, ignoring a path entering from the left, then turn left, away from the farm, on a track which takes you to the top of a rise. Soon, at a junction of tracks next to an open grassy area (marked by

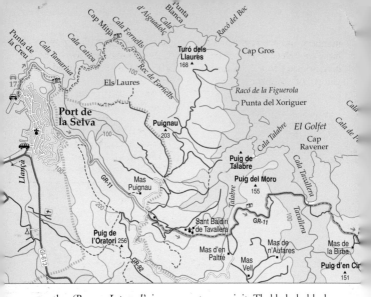

another *'Reserva Integral'* sign;
2h25min), turn left. A couple of
minutes later, as the track bears
right, descend half-left over a
grassy area to pick up another
track below, and veer left past a
group of pines. Follow this track
as it drops into a gully and comes
to the **Prat de Romagós (2h
35min**), a marshland with a solitary pine which provides sufficient
shade for a picnic. Tongue and lax-
flowered orchids abound here in
June, as do Spanish gatekeepers
and western marbled whites —
two butterflies which are
commonplace along many of our
walks in early summer.

Turning right and uphill from the
pine, pass through a METAL GATE
and reach the top of the rise, with
the lighthouse of Cap de Creus
just visible due east, shining white
in the distance. The linear
intrusions of white-coloured rock
to your left are pegmatite, an
extremely coarse-grained igneous
rock which abounds in this area.
Keep right at a 'CAP DE CREUS'
sign, cross a dry gully (**2h45min**)
and then enter a flatter, more open
area, dominated by vast swathes of
narrow-leaved cistus, where birdwatchers should watch out for
124

tawny pipit, Thekla lark, black-
eared wheatear and Dartford
warbler. Presently the ruins of
Mas dels Rabassers de Dalt
appear on your right, at which
point the track bears left and downhill along a gully to **Mas dels
Rabassers de Baix**. From here,
continue due east down and across
a usually dry gully and up a rocky
slope to the Cadaqués–Cap de
Creus lighthouse road (**3h10min**).
Here you can turn right and
follow the road south for 1km to
the 5h-point on the main walk, at
which point you pick up the path
from the lighthouse and continue
to **Cadaqués (4h30min)**.
Alternatively, turn left and follow
the GR-11 along the road for
2.8km/1.8mi to the hairpin bend
just below the lighthouse. Here
pick up a recently restored stone-
flagged path and follow this short-
cut up to the LIGHTHOUSE, perched
on the rugged, windswept tip of
Cap de Creus (4h), the
easternmost point of the Iberian
Peninsula. This is a good spot
from which to observe the spring
and autumn migration of seabirds
along the Mediterranean coast,
when Cory's and Yelkouan
shearwaters pass by in good

numbers, and you might even be lucky enough to see striped or bottle-nosed dolphins, or catch a glimpse of a distant fin whale.

which cuts through olive groves and then climbs up to rejoin the Cadaqués–Cap de Creus road (**5h**).
Keep left along the road for 200m/yds, to a sign on your left that indicates a short-cut path across the next gully. This brings you out onto a side road (**5h15min**), where you turn right and then left to rejoin the road to

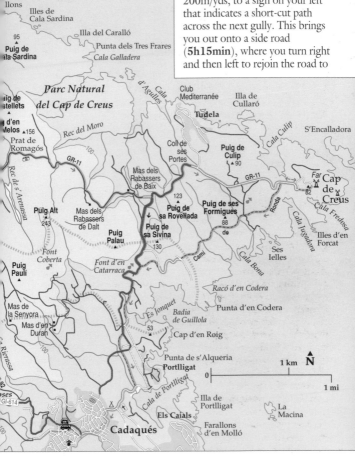

From here, retrace your steps to the straight stretch of road just below the lighthouse, where you will see a sign pointing you left to Cadaqués along the famous **Camí de Ronda** coastal path. Follow this path with great sea views for 45 roller-coaster minutes — as far as a broad track, where you turn right and then immediately left. Wind past a number of smart houses until a sign sends you left, down another stretch of path

Cadaqués. Look out for the next 'CADAQUÉS' signpost — this time indicating a path on the right which cuts off a bend and then crosses more or less straight over the road and drops down along a gully to the beach at **Port Lligat** (**5hr35min**) for a dip.
From the beach follow the single-track road over the 'neck' of the headland to white-painted **Cadaqués** (**6h05min**).

Walk 21: SANT QUIRC DE COLERA • COLL DE LA PLAJA • PUIG DE LA CALMA • PUIG D'EN JORDÀ • COLL DE PALLEROLS • SANT QUIRC DE COLERA

View north to Puig d'en Jordà

Distance: 8km/5mi; 3h50min
Grade: Moderate; a straight-forward route with an ascent/

descent of some 600m/1970ft along well-trodden paths, but the climb to Puig de la Calma (GR-11, then yellow waymarks) is fairly strenuous. Avoid mid-summer and days when the *tramuntana* is blowing.
Equipment: stout shoes, sunhat, cardigan, raingear, wind-proof clothing, picnic, water (there is also a spring just to the east of the monastery of Sant Quirc).
Access: 🚗 to Sant Quirc de Colera (the 104km-point on Car tour 5)

Located in the easterly sector of the Serra de l'Albera (see Walk 22), nuzzling the French border, this walk completes a circuit of the rocky ridge of schists which encircles the headwaters of the river of La Reguerada, starting and finishing at the ruined monastery of Sant Quirc (sometimes spelled Quirze) de Colera and the church of Santa Maria de Colera, both of which are currently undergoing restoration.

The walk starts at **Sant Quirc de Colera**, a cluster of semi-ruined monastic buildings perched atop a small plateau in the upper reaches of the valley of the **La Reguerada**. Follow the unsurfaced road north-west towards the 'COLL DE BAN-YULS'. Before long the GR foot-path short-cuts first one hairpin bend and then, at a second, continues straight uphill, climbing steeply into the scrub, here dominated by spiny broom, grey-

leaved and narrow-leaved cistuses, tree heath, green heather and Mediterranean mezereon, studded with the delicate white blossom of the almond-leaved pear in March. Now you come across the first of the YELLOW WAYMARKS that will guide you for the rest of the walk. Follow the waymarks steeply upwards until the path splits. Here fork right, now ascending more gently, until you meet the unsur-faced road once more, where you

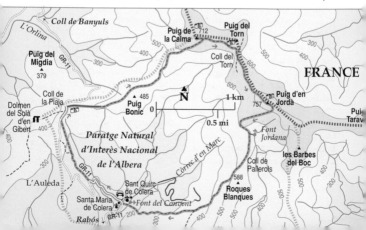

turn right to climb to the **Coll de la Plaja** (**50min**), a pleasant picnic spot with views south over the Empordà plain.

At this saddle, you *leave* the GR and turn right along a broad grassy track-cum-firebreak leading due east. This narrows into a path through scrub — dotted in spring with rush-leaved jonquils and a few green-winged orchids — and skirts the north side of **Puig Bonic** (485m/ 1590ft) before reaching a grassy SADDLE (**1h05min**).

From here the path to Puig de la Calma is slightly less distinct (but still very well waymarked) as it ascends the ridge to the northeast. After about 10 minutes you pass through a CLEFT in a rocky outcrop, from where the path heads steeply up towards a small clump of holm oaks standing out against the skyline just to the east of Puig de la Calma. Once at these oaks, complete the final short climb up to your left to the exposed TWIN SUMMITS of **Puig de la Calma** (712m/2335ft; **1h50min**) on the French border. Interesting plants on the rocks here include *Plantago subulata*, *Saxifraga fragosoi* and the thrift *Armeria ruscinonensis*, with wild peonies and wild tulips adding colour in spring. The golden eagles which breed in the area sometimes cruise along the ridge, and there are stupendous views north into France, over the vineyard-studded Roussillon plain (as far as Narbonne on a clear day) and down to Banyuls-sur-Mer, shining white on the coast below. Head east off the peak, still following the yellow paint-marks, to skirt to the south of **Puig del Torn** and descend to the grassy saddle of the **Coll del Torn**, marked by a yellow sign reading 'Balcon de la Cote Vermeille' (in reference to its views over the French continuation of the Costa Brava) and a white sign pointing

back up towards Puig de la Calma. The yellow waymarks are here joined by white paint waymarks, and these marks now take you south and steeply uphill to another grassy SADDLE (like all the grassy saddles here much frequented by cows and dotted in March with the low and unpalatable *Gagea foliosa*). Now the path rises through Pyrenean broom and blackthorn scrub to **Puig d'en Jordà** (757m/2485ft; **2h30min**) — the high point of the walk. From the top, follow the yellow and white waymarks eastwards, down to a further small SADDLE, where you turn right downhill towards 'SANT QUIRC DE COLERA'. This path leads you southwest under the south face of Puig d'en Jordà, then descends for about 10 minutes to yet another grassy saddle marked by a semi-ruined STONE HUT. From here head southeast down to another sign, pointing you right towards 'SANT QUIRC'. Just below and to the left lies the spring of **Font Jordana** (with a wooden barrier to prevent the cows falling in), which runs for most of the year. Continue towards Sant Quirc, always just to the east of the ridge top. At the **Coll de Pallerols** (**3h05min**) a sign points you west through a breach in the ridge, once again down towards 'SANT QUIRC'. From here the path is obvious as it cuts through tall scrub dominated by the white-flowered tree heath. After 15 minutes, turn right at a junction, to begin the final descent to the **Font del Convent/del Castanyers**, a spring situated just behind the monastery buildings. The latter of its two names is a reference to the huge sweet chestnut trees which surround this popular picnic spot. From here you go down the steps and over the bridge to the car park at **Sant Quirc de Colera** (**3h50min**).

Walk 22: REQUESENS • COLL FORCAT • PUIG NEULÓS • COLLADES DE PARMAL • CASTELL DE REQUESENS • REQUESENS

Distance: 14km/8.7mi; 6h10min
Grade: moderate-strenuous, with a long steady ascent of over 800m/2625ft. Beware low cloud, snow and, above all, the *tramuntana* (the French *mistral*) — a violent north wind which can make the higher sections of this walk all but impossible in almost any season of the year. Yellow waymarks accompany you for most of the route.

Equipment: boots or stout shoes, sunhat, cardigan, raingear, compass, picnic, water

Access: 🚗 to Cantallops (the 42km-point on Car tour 5). From here follow signs along a good but unsurfaced road to 'Requesens' and then to 'Cantina', to reach the hamlet of Requesens.

The predominantly schistose mountains of the Serra de l'Albera represent a surprising final flourish to the 400km-long Pyrenean chain before it drops to the Mediterranean, and harbour a curious medley of animals and plants characteristic of both subalpine and lowland habitats. This circular walk takes you from the middle-altitude holm and cork oak forests up through the high-level beechwoods and out into the ridge-top pastures, grazed by a docile local race of black cow with broad horns called the *vaca fagina*.

Start the walk at **Requesens**, a hamlet consisting of a single farm, a Romanesque chapel and a restaurant ('La Cantina', open for lunch only, Wed-Sun; ✆ 972 193081). Follow the track leading northwest uphill, opposite the first building you come to as you enter the settlement. This bends left around the back of the hamlet. When the track forks, bear right (yellow waymarks, sign 'COL FORCAT, 2.2 KM'). Continue uphill into glorious mixed oak and maple woodland, to reach a small clearing after about 20 minutes, where you ignore a track heading down to the left. Keep straight on here, passing through a *GATE* into a sweet chestnut grove, soon veering right at the first of a series of hairpin bends and starting to gain height quickly. After 10 minutes, as the track bends left, yellow waymarks point up two different paths to the right, just 10m/yds apart; take the *second* option and climb steeply on a path-cum-track to a wooden *GATE* on the scrub-covered ridge at **Coll Forcat (1h15min)**.

Looking up to Puig Neulós

Cross over into **France**, following the sign *'RFUGI DE TANYAREDA, 5 KM'*, and pick up a path (marked by yellow paint) heading northeast. This cuts behind the rocky **Puig Pinyer** and enters the beech forest, to reach a wall on the frontier about 15 minutes later at **Coll Forcadell**. Keep north here, just on the French side of the border, to continue to the **Coll de Pal** (**1h55min**). From this point you skirt the western edge of a rocky knoll, ignoring a track heading down to the left and ascending steeply northwards along the ridge-top into a pine plantation. About 20 minutes later you enter a clearing and shortly come to a WEATHER STATION with an antenna, just behind the large rocky outcrop of **Roc dels Tres Termes** (1128m/3700ft; **2h15min**), studded with clumps of sickle-leaved sandwort, alpine lady's-mantle and mountain dog-daisy.

Skirt the northern flank of this peak and bear right down to the FENCE MARKING THE FRONTIER, now with a road below to the left, and continue northeast to the **Coll del Pou**. Follow a track through a GATE, and descend across the frontier back into **Spain**. Now follow the FENCE northeast for about 25 minutes, until you reach another rocky KNOLL (**2h45min**) with a view north to the radar masts on **Puig Neulós** — at 1257m/4123ft, the highest peak in the Serra de l'Albera. This is an excellent area in which to look out for hunting golden eagles, surrounded by wheeling alpine swifts and crag martins, and with the possibility of summering rock thrushes and wintering alpine accentors closer at hand.

From here head southeast down and along the main ridge, following the now broken-down fence, to reach a clearing in the beech forest at **Coll Pregon**. Continue along the ridge, the yellow waymarks reappearing along with GR markings, until the waymarks direct you down into the beechwoods on the FRENCH SIDE OF THE BORDER once more,

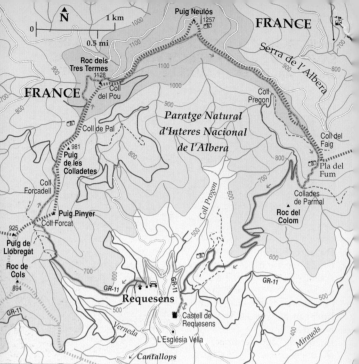

and then back out into another clearing on the main ridge. Follow the GR markings briefly, to the **Coll (Ventós) del Faig**. Ignoring the sign here which points you down to Requesens, continue along the ridge and climb the small peak at **Pla del Fum (3h20min)** for incomparable views south.

Descend southwest from this peak for 10 minutes along indistinct paths through a delightful open sessile oak forest to arrive at the rocky saddle of **Collades de Parmal**, where you should pick up a grassy track that descends northwards into the forest. Shortly, turn left onto a major track which, after two hairpin bends in quick succession, continues steadily downhill. About 25 minutes from the saddle, bear right at the first junction and then keep straight on where a track enters from the right immediately afterwards. After a further 20 minutes and three more hairpin bends, cross straight over a

less well defined track. After yet another hairpin, the Castell de Requesens comes into view straight ahead (**5h40min**). About 10 minutes later, just before entering a pine plantation, you come to a crossroads. Continue straight ahead, to a path signposted 'CASTELL 300M', which takes you through pine and holm oak woods to the **Castell de Requesens** (**5h55min**).

Retrace your steps to the crossroads, then bear left (north) downhill on an unsurfaced road, now following GR-11 signs and ignoring all turn-offs. You ford a stream in five minutes. After a further five minutes, keep straight ahead as a track enters from the right, then immediately cross a *BRIDGE* over another stream. Continue up the unsurfaced road to meet another unsurfaced road linking Cantallops with Requesens. Turn right to return to **Requesens** (**6h10min**).

Walk 23: MARE DE DÉU DE LA SALUT • ERMITA DE SANTA MAGDALENA • COLL DE VELLÍS • ERMITA DE SANTA MAGDALENA • MARE DE DÉU DE LA SALUT

Santa Magdalena: the chapel, mallow-leaved bindweed (Convolvulus althaeoides) *on the slopes, and cliffs*

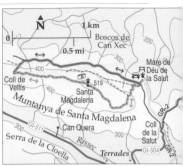

Distance: 5km/3.1mi; 1h40min
Grade: short and quite easy, with a climb of 219m/720ft. But the initial ascent is steep, and there is prickly scrub to negotiate in the latter part of the walk. Very hot in high summer.
Equipment: boots or stout shoes, raingear, cardigan, *long trousers,* sunhat, picnic, water
Access: 🚌 to the Santuari de la Mare de Déu de la Salut (the 13.5km-point on Car tour 5)

Alternative walk: Mare de Déu de la Salut — Ermita de Santa Magdalena — Coll de Vellís — Mare de Déu de la Salut. 4.5km/2.8mi; 1h15min. Easy-moderate (but you must be sure-footed); equipment and access as for the main walk. Follow the main walk to the 50min-point (the clearing just beyond the **Coll de Vellís**), where a small CAIRN on the south side of the path marks a poorly defined path (only for the sure-of-foot). This drops you very steeply and directly down into the woods on the north face of the ridge. After five minutes you reach another path where you turn right and descend to a track. Turn right again here for a pleasant woodland walk, which in 15 minutes takes you back to the top of the steps you climbed at the beginning of the main walk (**1h15min**).

The limestone Muntanya de Santa Magdalena, which peaks at just 519m/1700ft, is truly a botanical paradise, combining elements typical of the high Pyrenees with those characteristic of the essentially Mediterranean flora of the Catalan coastal ranges (for example, the Massís de Montgrí, explored in Walks 15 and 16).

The walk starts at the **Santuari de la Mare de Déu de la Salut**, a modern bulding of little architectural merit which houses a popular restaurant and bar, also serving the picnickers who use the tables situated in the surrounding woods. A large sign in the car park next to a cage of hissing geese indicates your route up the 'MUNTANYA DE SANTA MAGDALENA'. Climb through the holm oak woods for a couple of minutes to reach a short flight of STEPS, at the top of which you turn left along a track, then immediately right up a red earthen path that heads straight towards the north-facing cliffs of Santa Magdalena. This path gradually broadens out into a track, but after about five minutes you turn left next to a pine splashed with WHITE PAINT WAYMARKS, to head up a steep, narrow path. Follow this straight over two cross-paths, to climb onto the scrubby southern side of the ridge (**15min**).

From here the route up to the chapel atop the peak of the same name is a clear, well-trodden path through the holly oak scrub, although erratic red and white waymarks will assist you in case of doubt.

At the **Ermita de Santa Magdalena** (**30min**) you are rewarded with 360-degree views, including the scenarios of over half the walks in this book. The north-facing cliffs around the base of the *ermita* are adorned with a profusion of *Hormathophylla spinosa* and tufted catchfly, familiar from the Montgrí (Walk 15).

From here, pick up an indistinct path that runs westwards from just below the chapel (on its southern side), to continue along the top of the ridge — fighting your way through the scrub and down towards an obvious SADDLE.

With care, approach the edge of the cliff, to look for the dramatic rosettes and flowers of Pyrenean saxifrage — at the easternmost and lowest locality of its known distribution — and the purple flowers of ramonda, also at its eastern limit, both of which are essentially montane species.

Once down at the **Coll de Vellís** (**45min**), continue west along the path through taller scrub, to a clearing (**50min**; *the Alternative walk turns right here*). In March and April this open area is carpeted with the purple or yellow flowers of *Iris lutescens*, again familiar from the Montgrí. From here retrace your steps to the **Santuari de la Mare de Déu de la Salut** (**1h40min**).

Photograph: Pyrenean saxifrage (Saxifraga longifolia)

● Index

Geographical names comprise the only entries in this index; for non-geographical subjects, see Contents, page 3. A page number in *italic type* indicates a map; **bold type** refers to a photograph. Both of these may be in addition to a text reference on the same page.

TRANSPORT TIMETABLES

On the reverse of the touring map you will find transport timetables for all the walks in the book (except for the frequent city trains serving Walks 1, 2, 3 and 5, which are too numerous to list; these are shown at the top of the walk). The timetables printed in this book were valid at time of writing, but obtain the latest details from the nearest tourist information office, *being especially careful to check the winter/summer timetable changes*.

Bus times vary according to the day of the week and month of the year. Be sure to take into account the following:

- are you planning to travel on a weekend or working day?
- are winter or summer timetables in force?
- is it a public holiday?
- is it school/university term time?
- are you giving yourself enough time for a connection?
- have you given yourself enough time to find the bus stop/station?

Below is a key to timetable numbers for each walk. *Note that not all walks can be reached by public transport.*

Walk 1 See access at the start of the walk, then by from Gavà to Mare de Déu de Bruguers: **Timetable 1**

Walk 2 See access instructions in walk.

Walk 3 See access instructions in walk.

Walk 4 Terrassa to the Coll d'Estenalles: **Timetables 2, 2a**

Walk 5 Barcelona to Riells del Fai: **Timetables 3, 3a**

Walk 6 Access from Barcelona to Sant Celoni by : **Timetable 17** then by to Santa Fe: **Timetable 4**

Walk 8 Girona to Sant Aniol de Finestres: **Timetable 5**

Walk 11 Accessible by from Girona to Olot: **Timetables 6, 6a** or by from Barcelona to Olot: **Timetables 7, 7a**

Walk 12 Accessible by from Olot: **Timetable 7c**

Walk 13 Accessible by from Girona to La Bisbal: **Timetable 8** or by from Figueres to La Bisbal: **Timetable 9**. For access from Barcelona see **Timetable 18** (Barcelona — Girona — Figueres main line)

Walk 14 Accessible by from Barcelona to Palafrugell: **Timetable 10** or by from Girona to Palafrugell: **Timetable 8**

Walk 15 Barcelona to Torroella de Montgrí: **Timetable 11** or Girona to Torroella de Montgrí: **Timetable 12**

Walk 16 Torroella de Montgrí to L'Estartit: **Timetable 12a** (see also Timetable 12)

Walk 17 from Barcelona to Castelló d'Empúries: **Timetable 13**, or from Figueres to Castelló d'Empúries: **Timetable 14**, or from Girona to Castelló d'Empúries: **Timetable 15**

Walk 20 from Barcelona to Cadaqués: **Timetable 13**, or from Girona to Cadaqués: **Timetable 15**, or from Figueres to Cadaqués: **Timetable 14**, or from Figueres to Port de la Selva: **Timetable 16**

Main line service Barcelona — Girona — Figueres: **Timetable 18**